DIÓNYSOS

~ NATURE WITHOUT INSTINCT ~

SAINT JULIAN PRESS

Praise for *DIÓNYSOS: Nature Without Instinct*

Kevin McGrath's *Diónysos: Nature Without Instinct* unfolds in the liminal spaces between instinct and intellect, order and chaos, and life and death. Like the masked dancer depicted in its title, this work moves with fluid grace, transitioning between myth and philosophy, poetry and psychology, guiding readers into the deep, uncharted waters of the human psyche.

Diónysos, the wild god of revelry and ruin, appears here as both a mythological figure and a living presence—a force that dismantles and remakes. McGrath challenges us to recognize this restless energy in our lives, to see how the impulse toward destruction drives creation, and how the earth must be plowed and broken first before the new crop can rise. His lyrical and watchful prose guides us through the landscapes of classical literature and contemporary thought, revealing that the Dionysian force is not merely an artifact of ancient religion but a vital, necessary element of being alive.

Like the finest teachers and preachers, McGrath does not provide easy answers or try to tame the wildness he describes. Instead, he invites us into the mystery itself, encouraging us to dwell in paradox, recognize the sacred within disruption, and perhaps hear the voice of God in the ecstatic, the unpredictable, and the untamed.

Reading *Diónysos: Nature Without Instinct* unsettles and stirs, refusing to let us rest. It urges us toward deeper truths, toward the trembling edge of what we think we know, offering a perspective that bridges the ancient and the astoundingly new.

—Ron Starbuck, Publisher
Saint Julian Press

$\mathcal{D}$IÓNYSOS

~ NATURE WITHOUT INSTINCT ~

Kevin McGRATH

SAINT JULIAN PRESS
HOUSTON

Published by
SAINT JULIAN PRESS, Inc.
2053 Cortlandt, Suite 200
Houston, Texas 77008

www.saintjulianpress.org

Print ISBN-13: 978-1-955194-43-3
eBook ISBN-13: 978-1-955194-44-0
Library of Congress Control Number: 2025934109

Cover Art Credit: Ron Starbuck
Author Photo Credit: Akos Szilvasi

CONTENTS

To D.P.M.

Between instinct and speech there is death
So we oscillate in time
Stepping backwards and forwards
In solitary unison ...

DIÓNYSOS

~ NATURE WITHOUT INSTINCT ~

TEN PORTRAITS OF
THE NATURE OF PSYCHE

DIÓNYSOS, the masked dancer, is one who shifts subjectivity simply by a change of *persona* or visage and this is the nature of such pluperfect urge: that ability to move and to direct yet without the undeviating aim or precision which is usual for such reflexive behaviour. As a necessary corollary to this there exists a unique passion in the human psyche that drives us toward *stasis* and immobility, an energy or mental force that is the contrary to all that is erotic. Here, death is a phenomenon that is brief and imperceptible for like sexual union death is profoundly transitory and ephemeral.

This agency of invisible death always causes us to dismantle and destabilise what we accomplish in life or time; Diónysos is the name of the psychic principle which prepares us for new metaphor and narrative, what some might entitle *Todestrieb* or the pulse and 'drive towards death' which is paradoxically so profoundly creative and original. For without this necessary condition of entropy there can be no innovative act and in an obverse and simultaneous sense this then becomes a situation of nature without instinct.

This discreet dynamism of the archaic figure of Diónysos is destructive and disordering of the moribund and sclerotic and yet paradoxically, this imperative kind of transformation, this unbecoming is profoundly stimulating and in fact restorative of life. In agriculture, the fields are ploughed and seeded in late autumn just before the deathliness of winter comes to lie upon the land, until spring and its sacrificial or festal time of renewal.

Between the limitless world of nature and compulsion, where animal voices are impersonal and indistinct, and the world of human language and culture, there exists a psychic area that is both energetically creative and yet which is correspondingly destructive insofar as it cannot in any fashion be controlled or sustained. However, admixture is possible and this admission is the form of what once received the title of ancient Bacchus.

Mental travellers, those companions of the epiphanic Diónysos who have moved from the terrestrial towards the world of the psyche, eventually approach—both in imagination and then in physiological reality—the place of death where there exists no sign: that measure which establishes counterpoint to all our perception in life and which is the initial and metaphorical germ of anxiety. Our conception of death is the one landmark which pronounces the passage of days and time for death is the great criterion and is the source of all that we are aware of as discrete. To dramatise such an agency is to summon the image of Bromius, a situation that is neither verbal nor physiologically imperative.

This was the dilemma of the brilliant and charismatic Achilles in that he, the most potent and dynamic of all heroes should simultaneously enjoy such a vision of pure and implacable stillness. For him, that state of quietude was also the condition of *fame*, fame as a circumstance of knowledge rather than anything to be received. For ironically, if one is so true then life possesses tremendous ambiguity and ambivalence insofar as experience cannot ever equalise that vision of truth. Amplifying this, the discharge of human intimacy often receives the same terminology of metaphor as is ascribed to death when the erotic and the thanatic exchange similar words in that they simulate the production of mental or verbal imagery. Sappho was adept upon this margin.

Nowadays this Achillean view avoids us, for in modern cities we are only human and the quality of sublimity evades us, that attribute which is essential to all apperception, Diónysos being the ace of apperception. It is rural place and the spatial properties of *locus* which offer us the cursory apprehension of what can be termed as the unconditional and unqualified: a material sensibility or focus akin to gracious love. Our contemporary bucolic places are thus antinomian in how they admit us as witnesses and their view can be expressed visually or musically but not through verbal language apart from via the lens of metaphor. For Achilles, death was an impeccable mystery that always evaded location or any stable quality and in that sense the archaic fields of

Troy became a unique playground of cosmic effort, of repeated creation and destruction.

Dionysos, as expressed in the Homeric Hymn, is someone who in terms of identity is constantly labile and changeful; this is akin to the deity Poseidon in Scroll XIII of the Homeric Iliad or the perpetually versatile character and speaker Odysseus in his own epic. The extension of possible masking is infinitely creative yet, for Achilles, such disguise was impossible and that was the territory of his terrific grief.

Everyone has knowledge of our inwardly irrational mental life that is unable to be expressed through reasonable language: this is undeniable and much of human thought in fact—our inner practice—is of such an unspoken nature. This nebulous zone of interior being at times receives the benefit of metaphor but for the most part it remains obscure and profound, beyond the manifest yet fully charged with affect. We barely possess an idea of our thought in fact for the true genius of thinking does not reveal itself for it has no character which to express. This is the fictional solitude of Dionysos, this untitled and unspeakable terrain which inhabits us all.

Perhaps our only possible freedom from death lies in speech, how we use words and their syntax; for then we achieve the most that it available to human consciousness, yet much else remains. It is only in our acceptance of the valour of speech—say, in our promises or avowals—that we might extend upon a realm of possibility and maximum balance, when duality actually becomes engaged, personally and temporally. In our promise lies our freedom, and, I would aver, the being of virtue, the potential for full individual and surpassing humanity. It is there that we human creatures might overstep the fragile and thoroughly transitory margins of our being and it is there that we might at times glimpse *the masked dancer.*

I I

SIGNS are the elements that compose all consciousness and yet, what is that reversion which constantly draws us to water and its solution? In lakes, rivers, seas we partake of a thirst which is not material but primitive and aesthetic, satisfying ourselves with the perception of a stable level and a simultaneous swaying movement of fluid, as well as the audial sensation of waves lapping. In or upon water the genealogy of our life was first obtained and in and from the sea our own beginning and our primary motives were founded. It was from water to land that we progressed as we evolved and we remain forever lured back to that anachronistic and ceaselessly motive source, our most initial metaphor to which all of life returns.

Walking down to the dock with a boat, slipping it off my shoulders and letting it rest upon the surface of the river, then locking the oars and testing the seat. each morning—as the sun, low and still shining beneath the bridges, rises out of Atlantic—I set off upstream. The boat, with its stiffness and lightness, passes silently over the dark current, the oars flashing and dipping like long narrow bones. Each movement is accurate and refined—one is dealing with millimetres of measurement and fractions of time—as the blades enter the water, generate an arc of thrust, and withdraw. The rower attempts to fuse the rhythm of moving oars and body into a continuous cycle so that the pulses become a single steady motion; to that, one allies the breath, allowing it to relax.

Rowing, like fencing, is a mental activity of precision, it is exact and brief and requires a certain *hauteur* on the part of the sculler if he or she is to succeed in competition. The boat is like a long narrow spear and almost weightless, built of carbon and glass-fibre, and is in itself completely unstable, for it only retains balance by virtue of a forward motion. The hull is polished so as to present a minimum of resistance or friction within the water.

At the head of the river, four miles upstream, I always pause and rest, observing the life about me, and, if it is high summer, breathing in the odour of lotos that grow along the banks. Swan, heron, geese, duck, as well as the many non-aquatic birds like pigeons or grackles, maintain a private non-human world up there, playful, chattering, serene and busy, discreet among the murmuring woods. It is as if I had arrived at an island far removed from the disorder of *homo sapiens* where one might participate in a life of equilibrium and reserved tentative joy.

The boat drifts downstream with the gentle flow and at some point, as the water opens out into a basin, I set off again, driving the slender hull back down through the bridges and toward human society. Once at the boathouse I usually sit for a few minutes absorbing all the details of riverine view: how light falls, the play of wind and its susurration, the changes of sky and clouds, the colour of foliage upon the margins, the solidity of bridges, and the slow distant pedestrians along the further shore. Those moments supply me with a calm which I repeatedly call upon during the course of the day, as if discharging from a battery. Then the boat is returned to its rack and wiped down, the oars are replaced in their stand, and one returns to a life on land.

Human locomotion made its first gestures away from bipedal pedestrian life with the access supplied by a rudimentary boat and an oar or paddle. Those primaeval aquatic vehicles were probably baulks of timber which the rower straddled as he or she dipped proto-oars like fins into the water.

In form similar to flaked stone cutting implements or the spears used in hunting, those blades were one of the initial signs of human development. Unlike the spherical tools or stone axes, those oars marked an abstraction in terms of design, a move towards a conception of things, although still imitative of nature in their linear pattern. Their shape was also the sign of the *aleph*, initial mark of the Phoenician writing system, that single downward stroke of the stylus which generated an alphabet. That character is the incipient indication of pure abstraction which lies at the heart of human consciousness: the figure or character of the cleft, metaphor of zero.

Those fundamental oars, emblem of a human motion that was not performed afoot, were the indicators of how the mind of *anthropos* shifted, via design, from an earthly existence to one that was mental and reflective of the world, rather than always and only instant and mediate.

The first soul whom Odysseus met in Hades—or on its border—was the recently deceased and youngest member of his crew, Elpenor, who requested that on return to light Odysseus perform the appropriate obsequies and raise a mound in his honour. Atop the mound Odysseus was to plant the oar of his dead shipmate as a sign of former life.

Later on within Hades and in conversation with the mantic seer Teiresias, Odysseus is informed that his own longevity is one day to terminate far inland from the sea in a region where people will not recognise the oar which he is instructed to carry: they will see it solely as an implement for winnowing grain. That is, when the signature of his person and being is no longer an object of recognition only then will the seafarer conclude with time: when the signifier receives another interpretation distinct from how it was previously known by the bearer. This potential for the infinite mobility of sign is absolutely inherent to the figuring of Dionysos: that eternal possibility of a sign being the nature of how the masked dancer might always quickly appear from nowhere. The resurgence of the deathly only makes this likelihood more imperative.

So too does the human psyche translate through being and embodiment, always seeking the perfectible or the animation that is able to momentarily depart from physical necessity and compulsion: that is, to innovate, leaving a slight trace of its many earthly passages in terms of these primary signs of life. Death occurs when we no longer are able to interpret those objects and when we are unable to move among signs and to adjust our ability to recognise.

It is not the case that one cannot step into the same river twice but rather that the illusion of durable motion is rarely surpassed or encompassed, and when it is then the river is seen to not actually be flowing. This is much as in the literary phenomenon or trope of *ekphrasis* where a work of art is described and there exists an apparence of movement; yet the *tableau* of a Grecian Urn or the Shield of Achilles is in fact thoroughly static by virtue of its artistic perfection or approximation to that Dionysian *hypostasis*.

The name of the bow might well be life and what it accomplishes might well be death yet as we are all toxophiles nothing really happens in time except for our occasional understanding and awareness of the equilibrium which contains us. A gigantic balance of moments in which we are made to wander and inhabit and occasionally revisit, like the river which supplies us with so much pleasure each early morning.

I I I

NATURALISM today is characterised by—in terms of perception—a resilient pursuit of an emotional quiescence and reserved harmony; it is a way of life that favours the natural over the cultural, the rural over the urban. One can characterise this naturalism as a search for the sublime, that which exists only at the margin beyond the bevelled edge of human knowledge, outlaw and uncivil. Then the naturalist might quietly approach the figure of our masked dancer and occasionally retrieve that cursory sensation which is so intrinsically evasive.

The harmonies exhibited by still life painting or *nature morte* approximate to this same point where a field of visual equilibrium is posed and time—decay and dissolution—is sensibly arrested as if an instant of apperception is clearly presented; there are no transitions there only a reserved *stasis*. By representing that which is deceased—either animal or vegetable—the painter can portray an invisible trait of immutability and simultaneously hint at an absolute and *supra-impelling* presence.

The landscape painter can, through a subtle use of perspective and vanishing point, manage to exhibit an imperishable condition which—spatially—evades the temporal. Twentieth Century abstract expressionism sometimes achieved a like effect but without figural representation.

The benison which a viewer derives from such works is akin to the mental state which the naturalist seeks out in terrain that is suitably unpeopled and uninhabited. His or her progress across such topography is pedestrian and slow, essentially thoughtless and without pre-occupation. The naturalist wanders this territory afoot, speechless and without willing any direction, allowing the land itself to lead the way by inclination and suggestion.

Ideally, such a person continues the peregrination for many days, solitary and unspeaking, sleeping out upon the earth, beneath the trees or upon the ridges or on the shore beside the sea. That is the ideal which emulates the hypothetical moment which humanity once experienced when it set off from the continent of Africa heading northward to migrate thence about the earth, establishing what have become the political—and perhaps genetic, if not mythical—regions of today.

Naturalism can be construed as an attempt at the atavistic, discovering coherence in the ontologically and physically weightless; it decries all acquisition as a fruitless endeavour.

Although consciousness is rarely coincident with itself consciousness for the Bacchic naturalist is in fact ideally the sole ground. That impulse to turn a flat stone into a blade or a tool is lost to us today just as the belief inherent in the mind of painters who decorated the caves at Chauvet is no longer accessible to us; yet we can still attempt to re-invoke those natural agencies latent to place or animal, arboreal, and aerial vitality. The naturalist seeks to simplify in order to retrieve, or as some would say, recall.

Naturalists shun and eschew the modern, the technological, mechanical, and electrical. Mariners, wanderers, travellers footloose and without localised identity, such men and women learn to attune to their immediate and novel environs and to modify their lives to suit such transient states where they might continue their *mimésis* of Dionysos. Property for them and the accumulation of wealth brings no benefit, in fact it only bears hindrance and constraint. They tread lightly upon the earth and seek no effect, aspiring simply to an increase of awareness.

The gypsies of the Nineteenth and early Twentieth Century in Europe were of this custom of being. They continued to avoid sedentary life having migrated many hundreds of years before from the hilly regions of north-west India. Their beliefs shifted as they roamed and moved, never fixating upon any one system for kinship supplied their primary sense of identity and the few manners that were indelible to time. Being so apart, marginal and often solitaire, there was an heroic quality that lingered about such folk, they possessed an inner strength and resilience which glided over suffering and hardship; loneliness was not party to their world.

In this specialist pursuit of life, the naturalist avoids the present and seeks out what is in effect an *ellipsis* of time. There exists no human community beyond that point and hence the nature of the heroic carries over towards what some would consider as transcendence. Such information is unearthly in temperament and beyond the paradigms of border and limitation.

Nonchalant, sauntering, without attempting to impress his or her will or volition upon other life, human or otherwise, the naturalist lacks all point of view being only concerned with how experience presents itself. He or she is apolitical and unconcerned, remaining emotionally disengaged, purely apprehensive and without transference although interested in all aspects of occurrence.

In the style of the Romantic wanderers or the bohemians of the early Twentieth Century who were themselves succeeded by the beats, the hippies, and then the greens and hipsters, they manifested an urban feature of naturalism insofar as they shunned the conventional and constrained. Nakedness, social simplicity, undefined sexuality, and a search for the natural, these were some of the attributes of life that characterised such men and women, typically young men and women. Pleasure was never to be specified nor limited by abstraction and in their economy valence was never localised but always a shared worth. That is, as with those early proto-migrants, ideally there existed neither limit, nor frame, nor capsule.

This is not a case of fatalism nor of pessimism nor nihilism for the mental livelihood of naturalism is active in its selection of an environment. This is the peripatetic consciousness that inhabits a field rather than pursuing any particular line of thought, as the field possesses neither centre nor periphery but only extent. Beauty is seen to cohere about the unqualified and the slow, the reserved and undemonstrative: it is the ephemeral and the detailed which reveals itself to those who pause to observe, quietly and without haste or preconception. Paradoxically it is this ephemeral which triumphs over death and this is the original Dionysian terrain.

The naturalist abjures time and judgement, is thoroughly receptive and uncritical and only seeks to become aware of what inheres in others, regardless of intent. Most of all however, it is the purity of an unspoiled topography that draws such ones into a deeply inherent world, one that is lacking in all mark of the finite. There, the unrevealed becomes obvious, quite naturally, as the printless Bacchic footsteps appear and disappear.

I V

POETRY is the singular medium of Dionysos, the sonorous voice which declaims and discloses that elusive person. For me poetry has always been a practice, I am not a critic nor an analyst and my life has been in this sense a practical search for metaphor. The eclogic has generally been my subject, the poetry of men and women and the vicissitudes of their desire within a particular and formative landscape. Poetry has always been for me an attempt to go beyond the timely or temporal bounds of speech and experience, allowing these to match each other.

The truth of poetry is different from truth articulated by natural science or mathematical proof or even the truth of oracles, for the truth of poetry is simply demonstrated by metaphor. In this respect, poetry is similar to its sister art, painting, in that both media only create illusions. At the core of these illusions lies a simultaneous sensibility for time and for timelessness, which logically is a paradox. It is this illusion of stability, one that is apart from time and dissolution which, paradoxically, is the situation of death, that Dionysian *venue.*

I have always been interested in the preliterate origins of poetry and the song culture of early lyric and epic; in a genealogy of poetry it is in the reconstruction of that early substance of song to which we might turn for an appreciation of how lyric actually functions within the context of a human psyche. Such a process requires that one move back in time among the recorded thoughts of those poets who are now long deceased, identifying and reformulating their mnemonic and performative ways. Yet how might one retrieve such apprehension, understanding, and practice?

For me, poetry is not a personal expression but rather an effacement in the interests of truth, a careful and practically designed *ellipsis*. Perfection of the form being the virtue rather than origination or innovation of form, the latter being more party to a modernist aesthetic which favours an depiction of the individual rather than a *traditio*, not possession but the conveyance of possession.

Insofar as poetry is neither how we speak nor how we write, poetry as a medium is more akin to how human beings think. In any ontogeny of human consciousness a problem is posed in that certain aspects of wary incidence lie beyond the range of language—either in a diachronic sense or in a more constitutional manner—and so require metaphor or metonym if they are to be captured and voiced. The actual material of consciousness consists in words and something which I would ascribe to the Dionysian, a supplement external to the conditions of language and which can only be represented via the masking of metaphor. We require these imaginary vehicles or particles in order to express our ideas and perceptions and the grammar of their relation partakes of a world that is akin to the organisation or abstraction of myth.

Much of the poetry of preliterate and premonetary song traditions—both in antiquity and today—supports a declaration of myth, and the truth of myth concerns not so much what is being said but how something is being considered. That is, the structure of this spoken or sung poetry is at times more significant than the sequential qualities or its narrative: it reflects thought processes—grammar not syntax—rather than the serial procedures of speech, for it is the temporal which governs how people speak and write, yet thought is not temporal.

Concerning this kind of vision, at the literal centre of the Shield of Achilles portrayed in Scroll XVIII of the Homeric Iliad, the poets depict how a king, a *wanax*, sits happily in silence as his people harvest a field of grain; whilst extending further outward on the shield are two cities, one at peace and one under siege. This king, I would argue, is an emblem of the real nature of poetry for in his observation he is morally silent and without judgement as about him the fields are reaped and tended by his people.

Here, where the solemn king is stationed like an icon of poetry itself, the picture renders a strange yet constant focus from which emanates all visible awareness upon the Shield; just like the central consciousness of our lives which only and always witnesses without sorrow or happiness and whose only emotion is that of benignance or compassion. This is the visual admiration which is a necessary first instance of human awakening, before bodily pain or starvation, deprivation or physical duress obscures our joy. We are to remain necessarily silent when encompassed by those joyous reapers as it is language itself, words and speech, which do the reaping for us in life, gathering a harvest of meaning and signification.

There is another component of poetry which we have not touched upon which also conduces to the certainty of the medium and that is a constituent which is generated by sound. By sound, I mean the frequent repetition of small acoustic patterns, patterns that possess a simple binary structure, being composed of either long or stressed moments or short moments. It is this temperament which conduces to the much of the validity of poetry.

In India today—as in the past—many people believe that the primary creative instance in the cosmos was according to acoustic principles and that the initial status of the universe was in concurrence with these proportions of sonority, in that the fundamental elements of matter or nature were audial. These patterns were called *chandas*, or 'metres', akin to the similar Hellenic tradition of 'modes'.

If a poetry today can replicate or imitate those original metrical formations then poetry participates in that hypothetical primary creative event and is thereby authorised by that initial standing. Moreover, if those metrical patterns are used in an absolutely correct and accurate fashion the poetry becomes potentially efficacious: one can do things with it for those words possesses an ideal causality. This is the reasoning which lies behind the efficient use of *mantras*, mantras being small units of poetry or speech that are arranged formulaically and used purposefully.

Jean-Jacques Rousseau, in his *Essai sur L'Origine des Langues*, spoke about how—in that initial verbal foundation— men and women did not speak but sang to each other: something akin to what one listens to in operatic performance, especially in *recitative*. Much like birds today, their speech was sonorous although not necessarily melodic; that is, in the abstract the sounds were either short or long and either higher or lower in tone.

In such an audial model of human speech poetry recalls a genealogy of consciousness when it approximates to a condition of music, *mousikē*, or that which is concerned with recollection and memory. Poetry then recapitulates a possible ontogeny of mental awareness and thereby gains in license due to that amplification of the form implicit in a human voice.

Olivier Messiaen, the Twentieth Century symphonist, developed the aesthetic of the operatic composer and political theorist Rousseau further with his orchestral *mimésis* of birdsong in his *Catalogue des Oiseaux* and other parallel works. For Messiaen, within the origins of human speech were to be found the tonal, accentual, and repetitive qualities which are so characteristic of what we mean by poetry nowadays, that formulaic and musical vibration of words which describes or captures unavoidably imperative human experience.

In a minor cave in the Swabian mountains of South-West Germany a small flute, fabricated from the radius of a griffon vulture's wing, was recently discovered. The instrument, which is at least forty thousand years old, had been finely manufactured so that it would produce notes on the top half of the modern diatonic scale and the finger holes had been exactly counter-sunk to achieve this precise attunement. We might presume that the performance of this flute's tuning was on occasion accompanied by singing and those words— without the melody—are what I would describe as poetry. This is what I mean by poetry, formally arranged rhythmic and accentuated speech that is both radiant and unified, song that is with or without music; poetry only lacks the narrative melody of music.

Listening to the poets declaim Homeric epic it is the sound of poetry in its recitation which—as an audible key—opens and visualises that world for us insofar as its syllables cause us and enable us to see in our mind both our own being and our external existence as an ideal representation of mortal life. It is the sound of the poetry that produces our thoughtful imagery for sound or breath is our most original and most generative of metaphors, replicating what we have once seen.

There is thus a convergence of two axes which verify poetry with authenticity and affirmation. On the one hand there is a presence of image or metaphor and on the other hand there exists *tempo* or sound. It is the convergence of these two trajectories which—I would submit—conduces to the trueness and certainty of successful poetry, and this is the ancient ground of its Bacchic force. In this light one might thereby claim that such poetry is profoundly theatrical.

Or, to express this otherwise, at this locus of conjunction there exists a frame enclosing those grains of human experience: there is a much larger system of meaning and reference, a superior world of signification encasing those details and it is by virtue of certain vehicles that this supernal envelope is engaged and the poetry charged with the energy and drive of that greater body. These vehicles go by the names of metaphor and tempo: like wires they connect and mutually inform the two spheres.

For both the connoisseur and common reader, if he or she is to receive the truth of poetry these connections need to be discerned and assembled and it is this assembly of associations which provides poetry with its honesty, a truth that is not so much a state but a condition and property of language. It is there that Dionysos—with a cry of snakes at noon—makes those opening and repetitive steps, the beautiful truth of sun and moon.

Paradoxically, in such a depiction of poetry art is not life, and the veracity of the poem is—from that point of view—meaningless. Poetry, in such circumstances, does not make one think and poetry in this case refers to no-thing for it is apperceptive. By referring to worldly nothing and *not* stimulating any cogent thinking poetry allows us to walk marginally beyond spatial and temporal refinement to a synchronically larger and less definite world and there to witness ourselves.

It is *oxymoron*—the true heart and soul of poetic expression—that so functions by dislocating our mundane and daily knowledge, both irrationally and succinctly. Death is hence oxymoronic insofar as its irrational nature cannot actually be apprehended except in material consequence. It is in that sense our most initial and primary metaphor and has always been located at the heart of ancient ritual, the rites of blood sacrifice and the hypothetical first action of negation: for if we can momentarily—in our thought and sensible perception—capture death in its rapid transience then that quick second, logically, represents the instant which simultaneously originates consciousness.

As Dante in his Paradiso noted it is impossible to speak if one's vision or aim is true and hence we require metaphor to convey such significance. Ultimately however, even Dante abandoned that trope and at the centre of the cosmic rose he drew upon oxymoron, saying something which is logically impossible and irrational in order to capture that truth more beautifully, for then it was beyond and outside of incarnate experience. At the focus of the Paradiso the poet claimed that his vision was such that, *Un punto solo m'è maggior letargo che*

venticinque secoli a la 'mpresa che fé Nettuno ammirar l'ombra d'Argo.
What he is saying here is that, "a single moment possessed a
greater magnitude than the two and an half thousand years
since Jason's vessel, the Argo, set sail on its voyage towards
Colchis, when Poseidon looked up from the depths of the sea
and observed the shadow of that first ship passing overhead."

The whole of Commedia can be read as a cartography of
the forms of desire present in the human psyche, the various
paradigms of love, need, and domination, and in this Dante
serves as a great *maestro* of metaphor. At this point in his poem
however, even metaphor fails to enable a representation of
his vision and he turns to that other more enhanced trope of
oxymoron.

For the vessel is named *Argo*, 'shining' or 'glittering', and
Dante speaks here of the shadow of that vessel. In order to
communicate what is incommunicable by the usual forms of
speech the poet turns to the conveyance of paradox: he makes
a statement that is irrational, speaking of the 'shadow of a
shining thing'. Whatever emits light does not directly produce
shadow and in his statement of the timelessness of his
situation the poet draws upon an impossible example, for
here experience exceeds the domain of human language and
only an implausible negation is satisfactory.

Taking this model of oxymoron one pace further, it is the
specific contraction of the idea of metaphor whereby the
irrational or the logically impossible is represented as a means
of introducing an idea which evades standard verbal

communication. The *black light of pure beauty*, is such an instance, where the irrational conjunction of two contradictory terms actually communicates the inexpressible nature of this particular abstract noun 'beauty'. Oxymoron is the furthest that human language might proceed in its representation of the mysteriously unspeakable quality of the natural and universal worlds for it draws upon an anterior and pre-discursive situation where the nominal occurs but without the grammatically and syntactically organised speech which would habitually communicate such an event. That is the Bacchic landscape where death and renewal are coincident and perpetually combined.

This truth which is made manifest and overt by such poetry is arguably—in its nuclear state—a verity which otherwise cannot be delivered in words and is it only via the access granted by the use of metaphor and its displacement of meaning that poetry is able to convey such truth, such *veritas*. These are the truths not of intuition nor of imagination but of experience, experience that is essentially borne only by an interior or impersonal consciousness, one that paradoxically is not fitted to the constraints of the material frame or human body.

These are not the truths of architecture and proportion nor of narrative paradigm or sequence; they are not the truths of geometry nor of any kind of pragmatic form but are truths far anterior to such axiomatic demonstrations of the physical world, and it is only through metaphor that these inherent and non-representational aspects of life are able to connect with diurnal and mundane humanity.

This I would argue is the necessary action of poetry in a culture, the conveyance—or convergence—of universal ideals and imagery toward vivid social awareness. These are the templates not simply of moral life but of the essential and perfect lattice of our conscient being, the weightless and invisible structures within which or upon which all of our historical knowing and emotion are fitted and transformed into worldly effect.

When such validity becomes absent from life—as in many modernist and urban settings—there is generated a terrific and potentially destructive discontent. In the Euripidean drama the Bacchai a cruelly impious and delusional political order is destroyed by such a popular and theatrically feminine reaction of this nature. Diónysos only rejuvenates via such declamation and singing, where sound and image achieve perfect union.

The truth of poetry however, can only be destined to lapse and the question of the 'truth of the poets' concerns more a case of how to distinguish the poets rather than the poetry: for, as the Platonic Socrates in the Phaedo observes, "the *thyrsoi* are many but the *bacchoi* are few". Ultimately, such truth can only be idiorhythmic—idiot is cognate with this term— and once it moves upon the human tongue it begins to lose itself. The truest poetry cannot overtly disclose its message and the reader or audience is required to be initiated or mentored if that statement is to become available, for Diónysos is not explicit.

Yet there exists a form or *idéa* of truth in poetry which like the Platonic conception of harmony in the universe will always exist and cohere regardless of whether all the musical instruments are broken and their strings detached, for that system of ratio and proportion is indestructible and can never perish. The sudden incursion of Diónysos into a scene is only to remind the spectating audience about the supernal *harmonia* which has become indistinct and so forsaken.

As with Dante attempting to describe his vision of the *lume*, implicit and profound is that expression which must necessarily inhabit both worldly and earthly contradiction. Perhaps the truth of poetry really lies only in a vain attempt at thorough lucidity and perfect transparence and the nature of the effort itself is tantamount to the point. For me, the Homeric Iliad has always been the most perfect work of art that I know and if there is only one narrative in the universe to which we all attempt to imitate or approximate, then the Iliad reforms that model more closely and sincerely than anyth other work with which I am familiar: in architecture, music, painting, sculpture, or fictional prose. The arrival of robust Dionysos—appearing from nowhere like a flare—always returns us toward that one truly singular and utterly potential narrative.

Akin to this view and in a like vein, there exists the archaic concept of fame, that is, the fame which is not received nor awarded but a truth to be attained or achieved but the comprehension which constitutes this fame. This was the one possession of Achilles in life. Here, fame is something which incorporates all that has been considered above, that system of possible human knowledge and awareness akin to what the Homeric poets would attribute to the Muses, the understanding which informs poetry. Any cognisance of fame in this view is thoroughly *un*-becoming. This musical registry of knowledge includes the past, present, and the future, and also that which might be fictionally conceived and hence false.

The great mystery is what makes for the discrete in the cosmos and it is about this question that the systems of poetry circulate, a situation which is similar to the mystery of the syllogism and our initial ground of literal truth: the conscious topography of psyche. It is at such a generative instant that the masked dancer makes an appearance, distributing original fame. Hence, after his demise the ashes of Achilles were to be interred within a golden urn, one which Diónysos had given to the mother of the hero, Thetis.

Poetry has been an aspect of the human condition since our earliest days of walking upright on this earth and the intrinsic nature of poetry within our human narrative—in both act and production—is not simply archaically inherent but is a crucial and vital element of our life here in the world. To recapitulate so far, poetry is thus an expression that is musical and sonorous and is arguably founded upon the formal state of human language in its nascent condition and hence it is that poetry retrieves our initial and universal situation, a place where the fugitive and unmasked Diónysos is to be perceived. Just as the activity of walking and the pedestrian life of migration is deeply engrained in human experience on earth, so too is poetry one of the primary dimensions of our psyche, of mental and emotional life for it retrieves that *locus* of stability for us: an untimed circumstance where the creative and the thanatic are in active equilibrium.

Poetry in such a genealogy finds its preliminary occurrence not simply in the origin of language but derives from a further prior time of pattern-making experience. As with the domestication of fire or the production of stone, wooden, or bone tools, that incipient degree of control over an object's modification allowed humanity to reconform or develop its manners or kinds of behaviour. This original pattern-making that occurred in the human voice and its amplification—in terms of the generation of speech and the refinement and expression of emotion—supplied us with a nucleus of what we now entitle Poetry. It is these first prints of acoustic type which construe and organise human experience even for a child today. Poetry from this super-archaic view being the artistic enhancement of that same vocal process where only

speech occurs and where there exists no writing nor any other
kind of scriptural or visual record.

Let us now further magnify our discourse and return to
metaphor, what it is that poetry actually deals with as it works
to generate value and an awareness of human exchange. That
is, how events and emotions move in time and from person
to person, and even conversely, from cosmos and nature to
temporal and worldly community and culture.

There exists an economy of metaphor within any poetic
work, a system of images that connect and exchange value or
human valence that is both moral and emotional. This is so
even in something as rudimentary as *Baa-baa black sheep*, or,
Three blind mice. In the first piece there is a semantic contiguity
of five figures—between sheep, wool, and kinship-ranking—
and this enumeration is made quantitatively if not genetically
overt. Implicit in the little song are a series of exchanges that
lead to the production of worth where the tokens of such
verbal commerce and value are the metaphors. In
counterpoint, the Sanskrit Mahabharata is a titanic poem in
which lie encoded all the social and metaphysical conventions
of late bronze age warrior society in North-West India. These
standards are activated and dramatised by a system of
metaphor that runs throughout the epic: involving death,
weaponry, marriage, similes of battle, character, deed, and the
communal nature of sophisticated discourse itself. This
syntagmatic energy of a dramatic song is generated by the

unseen presence of the Dionysian with the poetry: the imperative, restorative, and visual and acoustic beauty of decease. Or, how it is that sounds afford to make us visualise scenes.

Just as metonymy is the organising principle of the medium of prose by virtue of the creation of serial *montage* so it is that the trope of metaphor functions as the founding principle of the medium of poetry by locating an event within a larger synchronic sphere of significance. By metaphor I mean the articulation of one thing in terms of another thing, of a woman in terms of a lioness, for instance, or a hero or king in terms of a chariot, or, more abstractly, of love in terms of light or heavenly circulation. This is the grounding vehicle of veracity in poetry so unlike the truth of mathematical demonstration or the evidential truth of the natural and inferential sciences.

So metonymy occurs in poetry and it is the warp and weft of metaphor and metonym combined which creates a cloth of meaning, the *textus*, the significant fabric which composes our literature or 'texts'. As a corollary to this, to any one metaphor there is always attached a tissue of metonymy, as with the ship of state to which are connected the sails, mariners, oars, storms, passengers, and similar threads of indication. This fabric is composed and woven of innumerable instances where values are being equated and an economy of significant exchanges occurs.

In societies that are preliterate—and such societies are typically also premonetary—there exists no medium of recollection apart from human speech or the record of an occasional astronomical event. There are sculptural and textile mnemonic traditions that capture and express human experience but these are precisely limited and non-performative. It is song which functions as a medium of transmission in such cultures for the truthful idioms of human nature, primarily those of love and death and all the many and various agencies which communicate these two actions or forces in the world: the seasons, like Spring, or animals like sabre-toothed and predatory felines. To pursue the genius of poetry therefore is to pursue metaphor and the possibilities of metaphor and to coin and to exchange such terms in the performance of song or declamation, so creating an appreciation of value among an audience. Those original *tempi* and images are only delivered through the immediate and at times invoked presence of the Dionysian.

Continuing to elaborate our aesthetic model, there are two affective axes for all poetic execution, the axis of love and that of grief, which are in fact obverse and reverse and are dualistically inseparable. For if we love we are destined to grieve at some point, and conversely, if we grieve we must have at some moment loved; these emotions are two mutual dimensions of an impassioned mirror or two sides of an ideal glass.

Love—in its inchoate state—is itself a metaphor for it is the unique means for us to practice in and to engage with the world: this is how we as knowing creatures move from zero to one in our awareness, thereafter becoming multiple and social. For if we do not love we are not in the world, although we can love a terrain as much as a person or an animal; Dante catalogued all the infinite vicissitudes of *Amor* in the vast cartographic scale of his poem. It is these metaphors of affect which allow our drives, demands, and needs to attach us to an object and so conduce to the generation of desire for a beloved—however that is manifest—thus translating a physiological requirement for stimulus from what is pre-personal into the individual, the dual, and thence the social. In Christian ontology this instant marks the distinction between the aniconic uncreated father and the mortally conceived and perishable son, mediated by the worldly but permanent mother.

The art of love is a practical metaphor for how we apprehend that we are not simply *one* but that there is a potential *duo* in the world; in other words there is this primary mystery of the syllogism, how we come to understand that all is not unitary but that figures do distinctly exist against a ground and that there is phenomenal separation in life. This origin of what it means to be discrete is fundamental to how we comprehend the nature of poetry and such is rudimentary in the genealogy of poetic art; for ideally, voice in poetry is that of one who longs for something or someone absent, a longing for the flair of apperceptive Diónysos whom we do not know and cannot even imagine and whose figure constantly encompasses all that we think, say, or do. It is the words, the primary sounds which supply those masks of indication.

True poetry stages this reciprocating duality of one and another, an oscillation or *tempo* which ultimately becomes the movement between one and the totality of creation, translating a vision of the beautiful by virtue of the clarity of words and the refined purity of those emotions conveyed. Ultimately these metaphors of love or psychic design—if the poem is successful as a work of art—are perfectly lucid and necessarily introduce the audience to the greater world of the cosmos, the universal that is beyond the distinction of both love and death and the language of those two conditions. True poetry will perpetually emulate this yearning of the lover for the beloved, for paradise is always lost and that craving supplies a depiction of both the beloved situation and also of the lover.

In the Hebrew Song of Songs or in the Sonnets of Shakespeare the lyrics are so composed that the expression of love or desire is transparent and the words are as if perfectly clear or perspicuous lenses through which we are able to gain access—mentally—to a world of resolved emotion that is overtly unspeakable. Such is the view which Dante received towards the end of his long journey—that of the *punto solo* which he witnessed at the centre of the universal rose—a solitary point that was apart from the temporal or spatial, being an absolutely gnostic or intellectual point. That is what I would assert is the place of Dionysos, the dancer of perfectly matched death and life, always oblique upon the periphery of those doubling and ambiguous conditions.

In the time which preceded the late bronze age—an antiquity of preliterate, premonetary, and absolutely non-secular culture—the terrain and skies and sometimes the seas or forests and mountains provided an initial ground for the formation of human consciousness: such atmospheres constituting the *materièl* or vehicle of what were breathed and immediate.

Before writing was developed our human understanding of time and temporal nature was different from our present or modern comprehension of such movement, for then human subjectivity was tempered not by individual perception but more by the influence borne by kinship that was always situated within a particular ambience or *locale*. We have presently lost our awareness for the pastoral and idyllic, for the terrestrial ground of our being and the *georgic* spirit of place which so inhabited late paleolithic culture and which generated its primary linguistic metaphors. Then there was not the separation—of the whole and of the parts—which dominates how we conceive of topography and its natural components today in the Twenty First Century; our contemporary and secular world has so forsaken its old and recursive *muthos*.

We might no longer peer into that ancient natural world, not cognitively, even though some might nowadays be still partially aware of how the unseen and imperceptible agencies of the planet operate and function: that is, in terms of the metaphors that signal magnetism and currency. Yet poetry, due to its genealogy, might barely retrieve some of those early vital conditions of awareness via its use of metaphor, although this is no longer what it once was three or more millennia ago when words themselves—if right and if the speaker virtuous—possessed an efficacy of their own accomplishment.

That was the world of what we now sometimes refer to as the *shaman* or seer, the Hebrew prophet or what in Sanskrit was termed the *rishi*, those antediluvian proto-poets who possessed and proclaimed their *veda*, their 'knowledge' of a corporeal and vivacious system of earthly life. That was a world along with its corresponding techniques of consciousness that we might now scarcely even imagine, yet their use of language lies at the core of how poetry was once practiced and that activity remains today within the still heart of all poetic aspiration.

In closing this chapter then, let us summarily turn our attention towards moral obligation. Since the end of the Second World War there have been a continual series of military conflicts in which the Western world has participated: in Korea, Vietnam, Afghanisthan, and Iraq, to name a few of the major invasions. There is also the dreadful hubris of the killing fields of Cambodia, Rwanda, Chechnya, Bosnia, Kasmir, and Syria, from where Diónysos the refugee, migrant, or exile is always fleeing. Climate change, the material pollution of our environment, and the destruction of water sources and forests are similarly forces of negation that are terrifically detrimental to terrestrial equilibrium and harmony. Despite all this however—despite the grief and despair caused by such irreversible losses—we do continue to possess a necessary moral obligation towards happiness, not merely as an optimistic situation of denial or foreclosure but as a consequence and resolution of a deeply philosophical empathy for our immaterial condition in this world. Poetry bears with it such obligation, a right standing that is founded upon contiguity with the Dionysian.

All the above does not merely concern the longevity of a tradition but the fact that the tradition itself is profoundly inherent and dynamically original to human comprehension. It is this awareness which poetry communicates: the finite position of humanity in the cosmos, the condition that envelops and sustains the duality of both life and death and of sexual congress, and the exclusiveness, constraint, and place supplied by our physical bodies and their driving needs. Poetry, I would aver, conveys an essential moral optimism towards our worldly being as willing creatures, and, I would submit, it is this which constitutes our possible absolution: in terms of the creation and reception borne by literal music.

It is with complete honesty then that a right poet might say about Diónysos that, *I pray that my aim be true.*

V

FICTION in nature presents us with a paradox, especially in terms of how in preliterate antiquity the fiction of the hero supplied an audience with truth. What was it that made for such truth in poetry? Fiction here is the origin of ideal death, that conscious human removal from a turbid Dionysian landscape towards a topography that is solely mortal, diurnal, and civil.

When in the poetry of Sappho we hear that 'an army of chariots or a fleet of ships' is beautiful, but for the poet herself beauty is truly only 'the beloved', what does this mean? For most of us have never seen an army or a fleet of ships and yet we know what the poet intends, just as we all know what a unicorn is and we could probably even draw one on a sheet of paper even though they do not exist and we have never practically witnessed one. How is it that these images come of artifice enable us to apprehend our validity in this world, or, how is it that truth in poetry can have moral or emotional effect?

Then, how does the connection between poetic language and affect occur, between the sound of the words as we read them silently, the images themselves, and the metaphorical force of these images; and what actually stimulates and drives those sequences? Psychic transition happens in this experience of silent reading—or in listening to a poet declaim dramatically—making valid an emotion that was not present before that instant. Likewise, what is inwardly experienced from mentally considering the panorama of a vast and organised infantry force or a squadron of ships and how does such fiction accomplish this? To go even further, how does this kind of illusion possess what becomes moral valence or force, and in Greek antiquity it was this which led to the community eventually worshipping a figure like Achilles.

I think for those archaic and classical Greeks who lived in a completely non-secular world that the worship of heroic Achilles was an action that demonstrated or expressed a truth which pre-existed in the universe, an agency in the universe that was even greater than destiny. For Greek antiquity the Homeric Iliad was a poem about an unmentionable and unstated cosmic force to which all must submit in both love and death, and this would also include the deities themselves. The fiction of the hero Achilles both constellated and synthesised this understanding of the universe.

There is also moral truth embodied by the conventions which we all live by and even human consciousness—because it is composed by language—is organised according to the usage and ruling of signal words and is not in fact materially truthful.

Poetry is the only medium toward this kind of Dionysian truth, an invisible point which occurs between the heart and the breath, although a painter, musician, or architect might argue otherwise. The perfection of metaphor allows us a little closer to the order of not only things but also of ideas and ideals, for all words are essentially, phonetically, and actually metaphorical: and not just as tropes, insofar as language is not substantial. For instance, when the poet proposes the question, *writing or life*, what does this distinction indicate, for the phrase implies that life is apart from writing. In that case where does writing derive from and whence is its creation for both terms imply and derive from consciousness and consciousness is simply and only a medium exposed by words.

This well-masked origin that lies within the domain of language in the world is a stream, a conduit of thought and emotion and of information which has consequence, it is not some static fount. As all human consciousness is substantiated by language or the manner in which we think in terms of words, those phonemes secure a metaphorical weight in how a signifier empowers a signified: the sound of the word 'pen' only indicates a material object *ad infinitum* and retrogressively for we can never actually reach the true pen via speech as we might only progress through further literal indicators. In this, words are merely fictional copies of an hypostatic original.

Certainly for Achilles, and let us recall that he and the old charioteer Phoinix are the only two poets who speak as poets in the epic, death is the great criterion and it is that presence— or shall we say that absolute and unique absence—which informs the epic song with its reality or what I consider to be its success and efficacy as a poem. Let us recall that at the close of his life the material remains of Achilles were returned to a shining vessel which was once donated by the masked dancer.

So how is humanity to be connected—in terms of language— beyond time and place? Perhaps we might observe this in the conception of the Homeric poets—in their Iliad poem— which represents a universe where warrior endeavour encounters certain fields that limit its temporal existence. We are fortunate to have evidence about hero cult in antiquity which reinforces this figure of heroic autonomy, indicating for us the not simply superhuman aspects of heroic life but also the supernatural aspect of such mortal vigour which existed in the world after the death of a hero. That deathly place was activated and invigorated by the work and efficiency of sung poetry.

Where does the relevance of truth enter into this model then? I am purposefully not addressing here all the occasions in the poem that concern human affection and the vicissitudes of emotional unity that occur between two individuals—Priam and his son, Hecuba and her son, Andromache and her husband, Helen and Paris, Briseis and the concubines and their slain menfolk, and between Zeus and Hera—as there is much love and expressed affection in the epic. The love and admiration which occurs between human beings is of a particular quality of truthfulness, arguably laid upon physiological or genetic reasoning, yet we might go further than such affective representation; and let us here remember that Diónysos is not erotic.

The ordeal of Achilles—not merely in the loss of his charioteer Patroclus, but in his direct awareness of his own imminent demise despite his own superlative physical and martial prowess—charges the poem with the force of its own conditions: that is, the power of song to become both constitutive of further human experience and thus actually indestructible. This is the ultimate validity of the poem, in terms of how poetry activates truth or how it was that metaphor generated veracity, and of—although not so apparent to us—how the simply and perfectly acoustic caused a certain emotional and phenomenal understanding of both the nature and operation of humanity within an unworldly setting.

Set deep in the basis of the human psyche lies an impulse that marks our most initial and primary effort: that is the urge to repeat or reduplicate an image or sound, a drive towards imitation and all that remains only in a state of recurrence.

For replication, by definition, is the signature of a situation that is a-temporal and unchanging: there exists no death in the repetitive world, neither decay nor instability, and in this there exists a possible approximation towards an absolute or golden condition.

In upper paleolithic times those early hominids numbered merely some thousands of creatures dwelling in eastern Africa; ten thousand years ago there were about three million humans living about the earth. What constituted—in their behaviour—that drive towards repetition, the attempt to reproduce a component of past experience? For it is this act which appears to be one of the most profound movements manifest in human conduct, occupying a margin where habit finds its onset and where the natural world tentatively recedes, at least in terms of raw imperative or threat. Valuation occurs at this point of the nascence of the memorable for it marks the onset of consciousness and at that instant the first human signs occur. Yet as we have observed, the sign is only a mask.

If the accumulation of socially accepted repetitions is what confers culture upon a group then what is it that leads to those original actions which reduplicate, what is that seminal impetus directed towards in the world? Or, is it actually that such an impulse possesses no direction and only seeks to cohere and conserve what has already occurred? It is as if that proto-human consciousness finds its rising in exact conceptual counterpoint to the uncontrollable threats of a rude and natural universe where repetition is on a scale that admits of no restraint or prediction and yet those recurrent states are what signify the genealogy of the divine. That is where the supernatural—those principles of nature—can be located and possibly identified.

Out of nothing, repetition is the only possibility, in time. Paradoxically, in the vivid and living world only death is absolutely and most surely repetitive and it is this irrational conjunction of the deathly and the creative that marks the imprint of where Diónysos moves.

Similarly, the use of linguistic templates allowed for predictability in human performance by reason of the exchange of thought and feeling. If something could be anticipated it need not be remembered: hierarchic order and the installation of relations reduces the need for entropic competition, haphazard and irregular violence.

Clearly the possession of an active memory was intrinsic to these occurrences just as memory is essential if an emotional life is to come into being. If we do not remember we cannot repeat and consciousness is merely responsive and purely reactive if not random. This is how it is in the mind of the *femme fatale*, that form of psyche which possesses no autonomous volition apart from a reactive gesture to what is humanly active in an immediate environment

Odysseus, in Scroll Eight of his eponymous poem, asks Demodocus how he knew about the events at Troy, remarking that the Muses must have informed Demodocus with such capable insight; for the blind poet Demodocus had never been that far East. Was it the case that Demodocus was simply repeating a song which he had previously heard or at least, heard in parts and which he then reformulated; or was it that the old poet—by virtue of his musical calling—had access to knowledge which was unique? Virtue here is indicative of 'power, influence, worth', from *vir*, denoting fundamental humanity or integral strength, the heroic.

For at this point in the epic Demodocus is being out of time as he describes in his fictional song a situation which he had not experienced yet which he literally knew about and one to which Odysseus had actually been witness. Hence the latter's question, 'how do you know this?'

It is as if Demodocus owned a faculty of insight that was capable of going beyond individual experience and imitating events which had taken place in the life of another. Repetition here—as verbal art—had progressed beyond the events of a single life and acquired the noetic properties of other persons, or another one. In a sense, an acquisition of currency had taken place in that what was being verbally exchanged possessed a uniformity which was common and mutually reversible. That is the mysterious art of true poetry, for it conducts and conveys value in many directions at once.

Again, we see that art is not life but something that is exchanged and reciprocal among living beings or at least those who participate within a single language group; for

unlike life, art it is not exclusive. It is a fictitious effort towards
the invariable condition or quality which constitutes worth
which approximates and proposes an order of the
imperishable and golden.

Hence Odysseus, who is so deeply concerned with his
own fame, is fascinated by the skill and gifts of this aged and
blind poet, thinking to himself, 'what exactly is he repeating
in his song?' For it is in the act of repetition that community
is incised upon thought and at this point the social is almost
completely absent in Odysseus' life, he is thoroughly
disconnected from kin and amity and his temporal being lacks
all recurrence. He is a wanderer and possesses little that is
satisfactorily repetitive.

This eidetic impulse is ultimately akin to how materials are
drawn into an attractive system of gravity, thereby
generating—in social terms—what is known as the
conventional: the essential structure for any human society,
habits of prohibition and exchange which are visually
identifiable. That is, the creation and fabrication of psychic
copies which are worn to conceal and screen what is in fact a
vast and terrific emptiness, the insensible void by which
consciousness is supported and which is the certain Bacchic
domain. The human impulse towards that interior situation
abjuring the constraint of repetition is what we earlier referred
to as a most deathly drive towards *stasis*.

Once metonymy becomes hubristic Diónysos is a breaker of these confluences, of the reiterative which becomes inflexible—and by definition this is not erotic, not in a practical sense—for this energetic presence is devastating in that all oppressive and necessarily fictional illusion is eradicated by a forceful disclosing and debilitating agency. Diónysos only works from within, annihilating outwardly and inclusively, removing absence and restoring immediacy. In such light Diónysos is the ultimate arbitor of the social, always reforming equilibrium whenever distraction and fabrication become excessive and arid: the sterile is then demolished by an act of unmasking. Like the zero in mathematics this presence possesses and owns no intrinsic value but its participation enables the work of signification or numeration to occur. Zero is simply a metaphor, and paradoxically, zero can never become repetitive.

V I

THOUGHT, to continue with the obverse of an earlier assertion, is that which allows us to identify ourselves in that it is neither how we speak nor write and is a process which differs markedly from how we read. If consciousness is partially constituted by how we think—with all the adjunct consideration of emotion and visual imagery, including those semblances of memory and the audial likeness come of written script—then how is it that we might possess an idea of thought?

Out of nothing comes something, a sequence of views and nominal syntax where nothing can be figured in terms of metaphors of light or illumination: a shining or gleaming which is distinct from invisible greyness. There, a cleft or obvious division is perceptible—as if two insubstantial rocks or stones were close together, or like that first sign of the *aleph* which a pen inscribes—and we are able to discriminate between the two. Implicit is this line, which in fact signifies nothing real, merely a primary or initial separateness.

The question is, what is the nature of the presence, the consciousness, or the thought aware of itself that senses this inward view of nothing? Or, what is this thought which becomes aware of whatever indicates the imperceptible? Within that awareness exists the barest sensibility of apprehension, of thinking, and there our masked dancer quietly and effortlessly performs, profoundly and formatively apperceptive.

Curiously, this view of cognitive action is founded upon vision, not upon anything verbal or emotional, and one might aver that the verbal and emotional arise out of this visual state where quiescence has been distilled to such an instance that it exists solely in abeyance? Abeyance in this case would denote a body of memory that is neither active nor with active agency yet is comprised by awareness.

As we observed earlier, so much of human reflection consists of a fashioning of repetition and its possibilities for imitation, for the phenomenon of intent recurrence supplies us with an initial ground upon which thought and thinking might lie. To move from that instance which is so profoundly frequent—in terms of thought—is not impossible, for the complexity of life allows an illusion of renewal simply because totality is unavailable to human comprehension, in terms of quantity at least: that extra or supplementary pace being the *locus* of apperception. Emotionally, without repetition there can be no love, and to be creative we must return to that hypothetical condition which precedes duplication: this is the quality which effects and makes eligible the true genius of Dionysos.

Thoughts move by proximity, usually by virtue of the links which metonymy provides but also at times by a shifting of track due to a confluence of metaphor, or meaning by replacement. Random thought does not exist within the stable mind and pure innovation does not really occur for there always exists another priority. It is not possible to be original for to be original only concerns retrojection.

So consciousness flickers upon a reticulation of words, images, and the diachronic situation of language with which we are infiltrated. Metonymy inflects us with an illusive sense of volition whilst impressions of novelty or innovation derive from actions of metaphor. It is place though, our material environs, that supplies us with an initial battery of metaphor, for place is the most immediate field from which metaphors are taken up and into thought. This is our initial source of stimuli prior to speech and so uncontained and without definition; it is that ideal Dionysian landscape where the maenadic dancer pauses at the boundary, ambiguous, ambisexual, and absolutely observant.

It is as if locality supplies consciousness with its first impressions, sensory patterns that are pre-linguistic. Over time, if a cultural group does not move from its generative terrain these images accumulate and assume a linguistic force, whereas for migrants, it is travel which becomes a medium of consciousness. In terms of the production of knowledge vision will constantly precede hearing and what is seen is always in advance of what is heard; or, in the case of poetry, inspiration will always occur before imitation.

Upon that foremost landscape the figures of literature wander at ease and in tranquillity and it is they who provide us with our paradigms of emotion from which objects of human love and affection depend; for there exists no destiny but the mimetic and the universe can only thereby unfold. Cognitively, we are dualistic in how we might proceed and necessarily imitative of either likeness or connection. That essential landscape—even if imagined—is the home of Dionysos.

Our life is thus one of constant reflection and refraction and it is only through sounding the depths and range of whatever is available that we might renew or recreate: two most rare and unusual activities. Silence and exclusion and the nourishment afforded by open terrain, sunlight and moonlight, simplify these mirrorings so that our own strange and mysterious intensity shines of its own accord, throwing up private, unidentifiable, and unspeakable forms.

It is the syllogism, that undeniable paradigm, which marks us as distinctly human, the binary of mental fission which is able to exfoliate and develop which sets us apart from life. That situation, with its brief corollary apperception, offers an initial ground for what can be described as heroism: our hint at efficacy which is both so revealing and so deluding. The syllogism strips us bare with its undissolveable pretence of discretion and all thought hangs upon this dual focus, upon this dubiety, a dilemma of which other creatures are unaware. It is this instant which marks the creation of tools and instruments, and this includes the idea of a sign.

Ultimately, our capacity for amity, for sharing and for giving, endows us with our real experience of time from which we never really retreat except in the practice of poetry and its perceptive formulations. Poetry emulates the order of thought, seeking to make the words hover like an envelope upon that curved and spherical original form where human consciousness is unable to recognise itself except as absolutely uniform.

As we observed above, fiction locates itself deep within the *prima materia* of human culture and just like the objects and conditions of the natural world it too is subject to time, seasonality, and the weather. For the perfect traveller or migrant who moves from one *locale* to another there is always a difficulty in how to infer and apprehend the moral invention that he or she meets and which embraces all consciousness as its vessel. Such is the interstitial fiction of human culture or how we do not cease in our thoughtlessness.

Much as in the classical Greek drama of the tragic theatre where masks supplied an overt codification for a spectating audience, the primary task for a traveller or migrant is not simply to understand how a culture operates syntactically as an object system of mediation but also to identify the non-linguistic signs by which social and individual messages are inflected and transmitted. These are the intellectual and the emotional dimensions of culture, in its devices and its grounding bivalence.

Then there exist the secondary fields of poetry and prose, of theatre, cinema, and the depictions of painting; the arts of music, sculpture, and architecture display no fiction being purely spatial in form. In the contemporary Twenty First Century world much of daily human experience is actually of such artificial kind: television, film, advertising, the world of the prose novel, and even much that is described in the popular press, for the fictive is a vital quantitative and qualitative aspect of ordinary and timely life.

The ideal traveller and companion of Diónysos traverses human consciousness itself, moving in time and through place as we count the sun; this is our founding model. So the first step that such an ambulant figure makes concerns an awareness of the natural constituency of metaphor, how it is that human emotion and conception can be expressed identically and differently; then secondly, how it is that metonymy supplies us with an appearance of serial continuity and the durable.

The great paradox is that *some people will never know* that metaphor stands on the threshold not only of all human movement but that consciousness itself—which identifies and locates such metaphor—is in its own fabric ultimately only an endowment of this principal Dionysian act of alternation, for thought will always occur as an act of exchange. It is at this secondary station where consciousness perceives itself as the source and origin of representation which marks the true basis or standing of all great works of art: the finest artists always proceed from an idealised beginning which they have struggled to perceive and comprehend and in that sense fine art is only retrospective. Yet metaphysically, that comprehension of the moral fiction of not only life but of the tissue of human solitude itself is the source of what some would consider to be the circumstance of despondent loneliness, dejection being a terrific source of psychic innovation.

All actors realise this in the work of drama, how to become another character not simply in terms of being but also in terms of how a *persona* perceives and touches other beings: the former concerns image or mask whilst the latter action concerns the performative character. Historically such an awareness lies at the core of poetry: the use of sounds, gestures, and facial expression to indicate and amplify the movement of a song—however brief—that are directed at a spectating audience. The performance of birdsong is a certain model here in that it is composed of unalloyed signs that are simply modulated in abstract reiteration.

As the radiant lucidity of Aristotle observed there is a pleasure in our becoming aware that *this is that* and no matter how possessive the *that* becomes we can always return to *this*. Such is the vast yet minor transition which lies at the institution of all mental congress, an oscillation or frequency which goes to compose our understanding of this place and its persons. In terms of practical humanism however there are few who discern any access towards this kind of moral fiction.

Our best icon or representation of the true traveller is the *femme fatale*, that one—either male or feminine—who is the owner or tenant of no specific identity or culture and who is always perceptive and acquisitive not only of manners but of affects and conceptions as well as the words of others. For them the constant practice of *mimésis* is all, for within their void there is little that is residual other than the bodily sensible and such is a horribly lonely, thoughtless, and vacuous situation, even at times a situation of mild and consistent terror which can be only be transferred to an hypothetical source.

The beauty and the purity of the mind of the *femme fatale* is that they do not know anything, in an historical sense they are the great originals and like the figures who appear in the paintings of the superlative portraitists—Freud, John, Rembrandt, Titian and others—they appear only in solitude. Such rare persons hold little access to metaphor and exist only by virtue of an endless gesture towards metonymy; they are permanently desperate to engage in sequence for they lack any duality or duplicity that is even slightly enduring. Without the reception of those metonyms there is no time and the *femme fatale* exists in an unseasonal and changeless world. Even sexuality for these ones is repetitive and without emotional substance or record, lacking a potential for series; their engagements occur only in a genital and not an emotional manner.

The *femme fatale* is our most ancient form of being and is thus close to what we now consider to be the supernatural, hence the likelihood of anxiety and terror, affect that is far more troubling that the philosophical seclusion which a witness of moral fiction experiences. They are fascinating people for a while but in the end awfully unwell. For without one single moral fiction there can be no movement of the human psyche and no adventure, for it is only morality which establishes the life of dilemma and agonistic judgment.

Someone like Don Juan has no access to the possibilities of fiction *qua* metaphor, there is no economy of metaphor for such a one who possesses no potential for any exchange of tokens and exists only within a dreadful *stasis*. The crime of such a *libertine* is that in their emotional isolation they are condemned to exist in a perpetually ingenious and inventive fashion, constantly repeating and re-inventing the same event until irreversible despair finishes their life. The tragic quality of Don Juan is that his ambition was confined to only one possible metonym, there was nothing fictitious in his life nor any hypostatic market. Diónysos destroys such mere outlines of the thoughtless and nominally human.

As human culture as we know it is made up of a reticulation of signals by which different societies manifest varying patterns of social and practical communication, there is no universal person and certainly no absolute standing in the cosmos. The truly complete traveller, like Odysseus with his hypocritical ways, makes a course through time and place only via the apprehension of those immediate to his person.

In this view there is only fictive thinking or the instrumentality of metaphor not simply in a pragmatic sense but also morally and spiritually; the initiating instant being that of sexuality where the distinction of simile is first established. In this view then the condition of genuine loneliness is a condition of true experience, being without illusion: those necessary planes and *fascia* that supply humans with an envelope of stability and efficacy. Such loneliness is without repetition of any affect and is philosophically an illuminated or enlightened kind of being, without the transparent frames that make for the structures of daily practical culture. Like Odysseus, the genius of Diónysos is solitary for that innovative or original awareness—in both perception and conception of life—is necessarily apart and without having access to the doubleness which moral fiction brings alive and imperatively dramatises. That creativity was the work of heroic Odysseus, facilitating his return home.

In the end it is the earth itself which is the origin of all messages, via its terrestrial objects, its seasons, and its weather. These are without moral force being so mutually and perpetually attuned and yet for human beings—reaching as far back as the upper paleolithic and further toward Neanderthal millennia—such natural forces need to be interpreted if they are to enter into mortal consciousness. It is only later with the advent of *homo sapiens* and the *muthos* of consciousness that moral possibility becomes a viable ground and such a geography is thoroughly apperceptive in nature. For the land knows of no morality and no moral judgement, its orders are always perfect and without a single trace of the subjective, and that is Dionysos. Hence personal awareness exists as the cause of dilemma and moral crisis.

This apperception is an unending and endless attempt to resolve the effort to understand what we are not and it is the best that thought can accomplish or perform. Its historicity commenced with the domestication of fire, with the fabrication of mineral tools, and the original tractability of canine animals, and then came the songs and stories and the divinisation of natural forces. The development of different kinds of human kinship systems was simultaneous with those first technical advances simply because both are founded upon a novel and gathering awareness of the possibilities of repetition, and those modelling arrangements of kin and kith were the origin of our intrinsic human and moral invention.

In this way deceit—in a platonic sense—is simply a quality of ignorance or narrative misdirection. The act of the novelist—especially the writer of detective fiction—begins with such an act of deception, which is pleasing to the reader, whereas the aim of the good poet is always true. The former works mostly with metonymy whilst the latter's skill is disposed toward the perfection of metaphor.

Without an awareness of the shiftiness of Diónysos we might never feel graceful, and then perhaps, not to exist is the best perfume; although that too ultimately becomes another form of perception and so generative of further thought.

V I I

DURATION, as mental exertion, offers a view that is elusive, enigmatic, and evasive to our apprehension, for unlike any spatial form it expresses no integral distinction and the witness must supply that quality if he or she is willing to admit the idea. Duration is that shadowy region into which the verve of Diónysos enters and then retreats and is a vital element in how the masked dancer apprehends the natural and human world.

Originally, there is only the timely and primary spatial cycle of shadow which is driven by the earth's elliptical circling round the sun, as well as—simultaneously—the earth's rotation upon its own axis, and that is in itself encircled by the gravid moon. All this provides us with what we commonly refer to in speech as 'time', this constant and perpetual transition of shadow, our principle ground for any understanding of duration as finite re-iteration. Duration in this light is an expression of shadowy passage, although without the presence of the material and spherical earth—and sometimes the moon—that manifest could not become apparent, could neither occur nor exist. For us earthlings the pioneering unit of this kind of durable measure is the annual year in whose frame all occurs as we travel through the rites and customs of courtship, lullaby, and lament.

Apart from historical duration there are many aspects and manners adhering about this term, in music, in architecture, in sculpture or painting, even in emotional duration and the movement of love. In all this however, the perception of a discrete temporal form requires an act of human artifice if we are to be convinced that true duration as an experience does not elude us and leave us simply with mere indication.

It is the practice of metonymy that allows the human subject to observe sequence insofar as series is the medium for an awareness of duration. Due to the proximity of repeated units this too is more of a composition of elements in a repetitively serial mode, surrendering an illusion of something briefly durable. There occurs an implication of what we consider to be transition yet this is not actually explicit for such is its mysterious elusiveness where contiguity only supplies an apparance of motion: the sovereign necessity of *post hoc propter hoc* is as narrowly delusive as any sleight of hand.

Hence if one were to assemble a group of say twelve photographs in a linear fashion beside each other then the animal mind would attribute an order of sequence to those discrete images uniting them into a narrative, one founded upon the linkage of metonymy. It is the nature of personal cognition and perusal which creates this unified succession of what appears to be consecutive.

Duration can also exist in a single two-dimensional monochrome photograph for instance, where a narrative is implicit within a picture despite the fact that nothing is moving inside the view and there is neither origin nor conclusion present. It is as if our humanly cerebral procedures possess a subtle apparatus which enables us to operate and to function with such depiction, for this is the virtue of the human eye. Duration in this sense is like the lines on the parking lot that simulate a certain order so permitting vehicles to be stationed in a reasonable fashion; we are able to fit into this kind of two-dimensional and static visual situation, conceiving of a story within a casual snapshot. Ultimately Diónysos will appear to stamp upon that terrain and eradicate the significance of such marks when they become cruel or impious.

Similarly, if we travel from point A towards point O, as we go there is a condition of conscious attention being given to that conversion between repeatedly separate places. In retrospect however—and all of human consciousness is founded upon and exists only by virtue of that memorable retrojective condition—there is no duration at all but simply a recollection of those uniquely sequent events which occurred between A and O and which have been conflated. It is the mortal brain which provides any number of units with development and consequence, the past is only a great concatenation of sequences occasionally linked by metaphor and there is no unified, whole, integral, and substantial past.

There is no past just as there is no future, there are only intellectual threads that attach to further threads and which are sometimes crossed by the shifting vehicles or shuttles of verbal metaphor: the *textus* that the human psyche casts over all that it witnesses by eye or ear. Human culture is, in this sense, like a carpet or tapestry upon which there occurs a common designation of mutual experience; I think of the community of language as being such an experience. It is here that the masked dancer stands revealed, causing a dissolution of such illusive attestation.

Those transitory incidents are actually only an alignment of one repetitious event, the change from a momentary present into a fractionally different and new instant present that is infinitely extensible, as with the fabled tortoise and heroic Achilles. Once that small moment has passed it too becomes past and only memorable and timely demonstration becomes a mere re-instatement of that insistence. Duration in that sense is simply the intensified concentration of a second of consciousness re-enforced by an immediate likeness, what in cinema is called *montage*, a carefully prepared pretense of coincidence.

Duration in musical time concerns structural episode, what we commonly conceive of as *tempo* that projects a recognisable architectonic form. In architecture, duration can be construed in terms of the proportions that are involved in or engaged by a building: a model of non-temporal or paradigmatic duration where the work of a human eye reads the *ratio* of metaphor, desperate to find access to harmony. Grammar, proportion, and syntax, all these sustain and integrate what are in fact profoundly if not absolutely disparate moments and events, otherwise we would be indefinitely halted and standing in the long poise of epiphany.

As with our previous example of A and O there is only one interval, minutely and interminably compressible, which establishes the retrospective fiction of duration as our senses move across the *façade* of our perception; that is the only hypothetical and real period, there is no other extent. In sculpture, duration is composed by the non-overt demonstration of negative space which a work logically implies as its obverse or invisible and thoroughly inviolable presence, its unseen shadow of space: it is allusive but lacks signifiers. Likewise, the idea of duration has no possible antonym, for Diónysos is stainless in that zenith light and without conversion.

In a similar manner the impression of duration might happen between two individuals and here any occurrence of duration is unique, matchless, and exclusive for there are no two identical statements or experiences that are durable: there is a transference of narrative only, ideal and anticipated. There are similar patterns or types but the distinction remains sole, impeccable, and immaculate; for without human memory—and this is different from animal recall—there could be no implied duration. The problem is that memory is not objective but selective if not actually inventive and it is remarkable that in human cognition, pictures—especially photographs and portraits—can give effect to an emotion of duration, can cause the affect usually associated with an awareness of duration to come into present being.

The *libertine* possesses no metaphorical access to this idea of duration and is destined to exist in a timeless world of repetition without accruing anything of worth. As we noted above, such a person has no moral sensibility for it is this apprehension of time that supplies us with all valence. The libertine might only move in a time which is in fact deathly as it lacks all expansion or momentum.

If it were not for the dead—the loss of a beloved—there would be no medium of interval for it is only that event which causes the human psyche to register loss as an affective circumstance, so qualifying the remembrance of the departed. This is the starting point for our apprehension of duration, for an origin is always, by definition, removed and absent; conversely, closure bears with it only a further sense of remove. In that view, duration can be construed as the mercy or worldly compassion of Diónysos where this occasion of the masked dancer is not simply one of either absence or presence, but also of modulation. The sentiment of grief is arguably the true condition or standard of our humanity and the only singular mark of how we think of living durably. Hence the figure of Diónysos once became the overseeing figure who invisibly participated in tragic drama, emerging and expiring in an unmarked singularity of phase.

Grief cannot enter into any market, unlike the feelings that encircle and noose physically human desire; grief possesses no fungibility, is an absolute in the sense that unlike sexual passion and biological drive it cannot be either exchanged or expunged. It is an indelible core, a nucleus that is irreducible and hence it is the primary sign for our acceptance of duration's impress in the world, a deception that draws us away from the circular and towards the linear; for the circular might always witness its counterpart or opposite, the simple return. This is not the case in linear distinction for the spherical exists as a situation of simultaneity wherein we mental creatures implement our lines and patterns.

The only true gold in all this suggestion of currency and endurance lies in our ability to move toward human affinity, toward the gift of human amity, with emphasis upon the word gift: that is, something which is given and offered without the expectance of reciprocity. This is not the protocol or customary giving that only creates and establishes mutual obligation, it is that old humanistic gesture of allied and respectable duration which provides us with our one conscient criterion here in life. Without that we become mere striplings of shadow, with a shadow's thirst and a transitory embodied lust which only exists by virtue of its lack of all else.

As with Odysseus as he finally set out carrying an oar across his shoulder, walking away from the coast and into the hills until he encountered a people who did not recognise such a strange seafaring instrument and who considered it a possible winnowing fan, so too with our comprehension of what it is that constitutes the periodic in our mental and emotional world. Only when we move across that point, that novel and Bacchic terrain where our habitual significance loses all its common and daily reference, only then can we say that we have experienced true duration: that transit from the familiar toward the unknown.

Then, however, there is nothing to say, no speech, and no one to attend to the record of such an ideal traveler; for if consciousness is apart from the sensible world only then is the experience of consciousness true.

VIII

WAITING occupies so much of life and only occasionally do curtains of light and tissue separate, and for a cursory instant there is not so much a hint of revelation but of communication, and we briefly exist *in parenthesis*, between worlds and kind. Then, all that remains are a few slight creases upon that irregular and ambivalent surface of recollection.

The unfamiliar is often a place to which we travel—in thought and other mental activity—where not only spatially but also in a temporal setting we are brought up towards a truth about ourselves which is not always available at home: home being our place of passing invention from whence all trajectory is necessarily conceived. At times we might describe systems of language and signs that allow us, by an art of mimicry, to move away from where we have been staying or where we were. We supply the standing grammar and go in search of syntax—the dual axes of our being in time—and all our action and urgence toward travel consists in how we consider these things and persons as inflection.

Yet there exists another medium where movement occurs, where motion is one of being elicited, and where the Bacchic messenger whom we had long awaited—perhaps even in decades of years—suddenly appears and thereafter changes occur in how we think and perceive. There we are not the witness but the witnessed. Lightly evanescent, almost imperceptible and invisible, such couriers arise out of nowhere and surround one with an explicit and enveloping *now-here*, hovering upon limitless and immutable air; colourless, silent, and spherical in an absolutely informative way and known only between the eyes. What they impart is not knowledge or anything substantial but a weightless and potent charge which precedes the embodiment of form as it exists in duration.

In these moments an undoing is taking place, and all that we have struggled for, all that we have made so much effort towards, the *pothos* or 'desire' that had ruled our days and years is unfitted and removed; for suddenly there is no point. That wonderful instant when equilibrium took us away—although untimed—is abrupt in its longevity, for the messenger soon retires. The presence of such an emissary is often only formulated in retrospect where the reality of the event happens in memorable recollection as the meeting only inhabits us through its recall.

As the curtains part or the unseen panels soundlessly and without forecast glide open the emotion experienced is one of satisfaction: *so there we are*, at last and instantly out of time, undone and inactive. We are received, recognised, and believed, and something is ensured as we return, some promise that is faithful to the future and yet more.

Recently I was visiting an exhibition of contemporary photographs in a new and post-modern museum when suddenly I found myself standing before a large coloured picture of hillsides and a small plain. There was something acutely and intimately familiar about the scene and I immediately realised that I knew the place: the outline shape of the hills, their conformation and incline was somehow intrinsically part of my life, available and known only preconsciously.

I moved and bent down to read the catalogue description of the image and saw the words Sha Tin. That was a place and a name which I had neither seen nor heard for about fifty years since I had spent my boyhood in southern China. Somewhere in my psyche the imprint from and profile of those hills had remained and I had recognised the distinctive contour so long after, although I had superficially forgotten exactly where the terrain existed. Nevertheless I knew that it was somewhere near the coast of the South China Sea, so forceful had been that juvenile impression.

Similarly, we assume that these Dionysian messengers—whoever or whatever they are—journey towards us and visit us on certain absolutely implicit occasions, yet in fact they are with us all the time and only rarely uncover themselves for us, undressing their untimeliness and drawing us towards them as they show off their unspeakable body. Sometimes they are singular and large at other times they are manifoldly various and teeming; their figure is always spherical however and numinous, perfectly transparent and lacking any occlusion for us who simply stand and wait.

All our exertions—because our days are formulated in time—are in fact merely a bearing of time and the only true struggle is to maintain consciousness so that we are able to receive the impress of such moments and can infer from them the wealth of wisdom which they offer; for they do not give, they merely offer.

Sha Tin was always there in my life even although I was unaware of this and certainly not knowing of how that visual silhouette of place and the two phonemes influenced and participated in all my subsequent thought and passion. Likewise, the messengers are always there, but not just within a life, but without it, enduring beyond any single monadic comprehension of existence. Confluent, generous, infinitely kind, donating in a most gracious manner, they are constantly attending upon us, and not we them.

One might hence propose that there is a necessity in grief and in mourning that invisibly encircles these nameless experiences which we convey so lightly and that, without a certain expiation, there can be no eventual restoration. The grief is one not of sorrow however but of benevolence and incorporation and the journey is not of this practical world but is one of speech and of the words or sounds that sustain consciousness. We work with language, that is our labour and only substantial activity and it is that patience and travail which extends itself for us as a sum of periods and intervals.

The messengers appear to us when we least expect their presence and all our endurance and application goes towards those moments which split the envelope of our being and take us away, adding to our latitude and longitude. There are trials and tests and yet the real business lies in our preparation of virtue and its manifest courage: the loneliness of giving more than we receive. For truly our name is *Aithón* and as the human spirit migrates across time and experience it is only the sanction of these messengers which advances us along the way; again, this is the compassionate aspect of the masked dancer. It is only when we struggle with death—mentally and thoughtfully—that we are given access to true life, and anyone who works in fine art soon realises this idea or belief of death as criterion and not merely as physiological demise.

For me, all of life has been an enduring exploration of metaphor or pursuit of the genius of poetry: in the Americas, in Europe, in Asia, and in Africa, and that kind of progress has always composed my distance. To travel is a means for approaching and for arresting metaphor: look at Joseph Conrad, for instance, the old voyager, and how he attempted throughout his life to understand what he was not. That *terra nova* was for him always a moral ground and for Conrad on his voyages the only true frontiers were to be located in moments of moral recognition.

Paradoxically, in this pursuit of ethical solitude wherein one might—with closed eyes—witness the non-plurality of the world, the condition is not social but mental and affective and it is there that we secure a resilient strength. When nothing exists, as in a perfect still life painting—and this is difficult to achieve conceptually for it demands pristine discipline and tensile rigour—then we are truly tested and yet we might only then accomplish our vision and briefly observe the fugitive and raucous Bromius. Ultimately, if we are certainly free and liberal we might only reflect, entering that realm of unwitnessed refraction so that our interior light might become stable. Such truthfulness or veracity of apperception is completely tenacious and yet without our persistent resolve nothing can be feasible on earth, not in terms of psychic manumission.

Friendship, meditation, and solitude convert us and none of these can be effective without resolute conviction: this is not faith but is founded upon experience and knowledge and that nature of immaterial vision. It is this which I would refer to as the *art of travel*. This certainty is mysterious for it is neither rational nor derived from anything memorable; it is a certitude which cannot be taught nor transmitted for it bears an unusual and inexplicable inevitability about its visual and Bacchic ways.

These circumstances underlie, integrate, and cause to inhere what becomes acoustically, literally, and aesthetically the place or occurrence of poetry and its versatile character of human measurement: that is, poetry as a vehicle or medium of conceptual transition, shuttling across lives, fabricating our daily love.

In such perfect invocation there is no entity and that is the work, to create and to establish a vision of all potential, unworldly, untimed, and never discrete. This in fact amounts to true love or the single kernel and core of possible human amity, that fundamental worth which seeks to exchange but only in terms of giving and not of reception. For our only firm meaning in mortal life—to give and not to receive—is the true labour where all effort is to be directed. The transparency of candid poetry imitates this and true poetry as we know is always led on by the psychic imprint of Dionysos.

In such action, solitude—being that is lone and sole—is not emotional but abstract and ontological, a state where we affirm our cognisance of others and our admission of what we are not. Those who possess or who carry no capacity for despond or despair do not perceive or apprehend this kind of encapsulation or infolding of knowledge, for desperation is simply the initial and personal ground of anything that is exposed and revealed.

So we travel on earth seeking the especial terrain of poetry, walking through wilderness and empty landscape or visiting those ancient sites—like Dholavira in far-western Gujarat, or Mycenae in the Greek Peloponnese, or the Arawak campsite on eastern Carriacou in the Grenadine Windward Isles— pursuing an authenticity of experience in a form of antique material reality, struggling to perceive the truly ephemeral. These are places, strange and vague situations where death is manifold and thoroughly extant to the careful eye. There are women's bangles made of shell to be picked up from the saline dust or small copper beads and thin chert blades, or tiny obsidian arrow-heads that can be unhidden and disclosed beneath those bloody grey walls about the Lion Gate, or beautiful indented potsherds recording the impress of an ancient fingertip upon ceramic fragments, at the waterline where the Atlantic rolls out its long blue visceral waves.

All these rare and disjected objects come to us from millennia ago and can be read for their quiet validity and record of ancient human attendance, for in these places we are travelling in time and passing through the unseen tissue and blind gateways of an absolute and unsigned dissolution.

That is where poetry begins, alone in an unaffected and untroubled world where the initial traces of humankind can be raised and admired, particularly for its stains of human loss and grief, in its burial and cremation. There we might be escorted by Diónysos to those rare situations beyond death.

For me, walking has always been a medium of thought and one always approaches those ancient sites on foot and patrols them as a pedestrian, for poetry has always remained the ultimate medium of travel, the only good *yoga* that I know and which is practicable: how we move from metaphor to metaphor, usually on foot and walking in regions—the alkaline desert, the blond hills, or obdurate coast—where in solitude there is a stripping away of our intellectual and habitual clothing so that we might receive some few loose grains of the masked genius of this round earth and sky; where light is actually marked with the invisible signs that take us away from the informed and fungible world and its bounds. For original genius only possesses one power of truth. Think of Charles Darwin as a young and unmarried mariner pacing the decks of the *Beagle* and pondering the qualities of material translation and temporal life, think of the interminable and exacting details which he was required to research and to contemplate.

Before we can comprehend these indications we must abandon our own station and its establishment and this requires terrific individual dominion and a mind that is almost athletic in its ability not simply to reach the margins but to

continue further with that veritable exertion: one that is
mental and not physical. In these circumstances friendship
with Diónysos is sovereign—like heart-beaten breath—for
the air of this world is composed of the myriad words of
exhalation which have been spoken for tens of millennia: that
is the truly perfect immaterial Dionysian body, its tissue and
matter.

In all such endeavor and determination consciousness is our
master and neither words nor thoughts go there; we move
with poetry and the yoking of our humanity with an animal
strength, with the hawk-eyes of limitless vision. Walking
among the powdery dust of those chalcolithic cities far out in
the desert, where, for instance—in the company of friends
who are completely unlike ourselves—we share an experience
of a passing and indelibly indestructible truth: who can stand
unique in such a sure void when encompassed by such lucid
messengers?

As with *nature morte* this is what poetry attempts to emulate
and to reserve for us, engaging various platforms and
conversions of metaphor to serve the incidence of perfectly
transparent images of beauty and to attend to them with a
near amorous devotion which is able to be clearly victorious
even in the presence of death. If we do not perceive that
unmasked presence then we cannot follow any truth, and
then, there can never be poetry nor belief. In this the patient
fire of alert contemplation is like a spear, an arrow, or a javelin

whose aim is true.

I X

MARK Rothko painted the Harvard Murals in Nineteen Sixty-One and they were recently—having been restored by a process of artificial luminosity—on short-term exhibit at the new Fogg Museum on Quincy Street in Cambridge. There are two other groups of similar work: the splendid Seagram paintings which are now dispersed among three museums on three continents, and the others—in the Rothko Chapel at Houston—that are more architectural than painterly. What follows here is an *ekphrastic* reflection on a mural room.

These six works are large views onto what is almost a prediscursive vision of the world, a pre-social or even pre-mythical scrutiny that does not aim at humanity but at *being* itself, a figuring of state which precedes both life and death. The gently radiant forms themselves are profoundly different in each painting and are in no manner repetitious: in this work even the idea of repetition is not feasible for such is the fully inherent unity of expression here. How Rothko arrived at these indeterminate shapes is a mystery and the aetiology of these outline forms remains undisclosed as they remain profoundly non-representational and unique. Simultaneously they are full of life, in fact that is all that they are, life that exists without embodiment, for the pictures are as if windows or frames that allow the spectator to have access to such an unworldly and inhumanly pure existence, or what we might humanly phrase as a purely exuberant Dionysian cosmos.

The pictures are not just conceptual renderings but are majestically powerful images that are able to amplify a strong emotional presence, an incidence of silence and immobility that is both pre-verbal and unaware of language: they communicate by emanation. The absolute potential for consciousness in these pictures is vast and motionless, insensible, thoroughly alive, and yet superlatively sentient. Here there is no melody, no grammar, no distinction nor resolution; neither origin nor terminus, there is only stillness and absolution, a faultless magnitude that is atemporal.

Not many individuals in this world are able to see like Rothko manages to discern, to actually examine slowly and carefully and then to be able to translate that experience of discrimination into plastic signification that can itself reveal such visual knowledge, transmitting the message onward toward another medium in the eye of the beholder. This is especially the case because what Rothko paints does not exist in the world as we know it, much as the portraits of Lucian Freud present human beings but not as they live and breathe but in terms of their interior and invisible psyche.

This is a *mantic* ability, a gift of the Muses akin to the descrying which the great poets are able to perform. The dialectic is such that the communication between this unseen world and the visual and conceptual sensation of the spectator occurs via the intermediary work of the painter. Gauguin managed to accomplish this in his masterpiece *D'où Venons-Nous*, but he continued to depend upon myth and the representation of those metaphors. Rothko excludes metaphor from his pictures.

To be able to understand the material world in such a light and to be able to apprehend such truth in the world is what distinguishes the most superlative artists. This is not a technical ability nor a matter of arranging proportion, perspective, nor composition but of consciousness itself, of being able to touch upon an unspeakable and *supra*-natural Bacchic condition.

The paintings have been carefully and slowly developed using innumerable thin layers of diluted pigment which give the works a subtle yet infinitely nuanced and dynamic texture. It is as if the surface of these canvases is a living and vibrant tissue of transparent awareness for the quality of the paint constantly and delicately varies across the face of the work; even blackness assumes a refined and perpetual activity. The modelling of the forms is lightly extensive and brings to these images both volume and depth and the dimensions are such that both foreground and background can be exchanged by the human eye with little effort, so shifting the object of the work and allowing the body of the painting to move simultaneously back and forth in easy visual exchange, in an oscillation or frequency that partakes of no timely measure.

The sparse watery curvature that occurs at the edge of some of these shapes sustains the implicit volume of the object so that it possesses not simply surface but also quantitative mass and receding silhouette. The continuously shifting saturation and pigmentation of the chromatic field lends minute activity to the colour which performs this action; thousands of small precise brush-strokes must have gone into the production of the pictures.

The non-representational quality of these forms defeats the viewer because all metonymy is precluded in this unique depiction and even the possibility of metaphor is curtailed if not occluded. Yet paradoxically—or even oxymoronically— the forms are completely vital and ponderously vivacious, they are definitely not abstractions but pictures of terrific life and immense vigour in how they manifest and express their mysterious and soundless existence. Thus irrationally, they are figure and non-figure equally and at once and are hence able to overcome or defeat that which is simply finite: the viewer in his or her sensible perception. Even death is by definition finite.

It is rare for painting to go this far and there are few works in the last two centuries of the Western tradition which achieve such visionary movement, for it is almost impossible to represent something that does not exist except in an extremely enlightened state or situation. As Brice Marden once observed, "Cézanne is the end of painting," yet these present canvases go much further in this respect in that they take painting to a point that is rarely experienced not only by artists but by human beings in general; for such a circumstance is not earthly and has no real place.

These five visual and profoundly ephemeral monuments—along with their earlier three oil-sketch works, one of which is even more extraordinarily non-representational than all the others, and along with some initial designs on paper—can now only be viewed in the light of an especially designed and projected illumination which restores the original colouring of the canvases. Rothko had employed a pigment that was corrupt and elusive with the result that the chromatic density and first hue of the painting has vanished over time and so nowadays needs to be artificially resumed.

The grandeur of the vision is such though that what the viewer experiences is necessarily phenomenal and ephemeral and that view cannot be retained and taken beyond the room where the paintings presently hang. The unqualified complexity of the images is such that the human mind cannot transport these captions of the beautiful any further than where they exist in time today. Again, this is another paradox, that such a vision can be so strongly depicted and yet the spectator cannot actually possess that scene beyond its immediate sighting and physical location. The force of the pictures is such that they evade memory or recall for the experience is only and absolutely immediate. In the same way no one ever remembers the features of fugitive Diónysos or what exists and occurs beneath those innumerable masks.

One of Rothko's earlier horizontal 'multiform' paintings was sold at auction not so long ago for between eighty and ninety million dollars; these Harvard murals—which are vertical in plan—are worth even more. Insofar as the pictures portray an hypothetical origin of consciousness they are therefore in an immanent sense depicting the actual source of human valence, hence the superb price of these works in the modern market. The work of artistic *entrepreneurs* like Hirst or Warhol are only tokens of value for the creativity of these 'makers' is not any way equivalent to the profound originality of what Rothko accomplished; they are thoroughly different in nature for the work of Hirst and Warhol is only mediate and not universal and remains in the capitalistic style of Marcel Duchamp. Even the magnificent compositions of painters like Motherwell, Newman, or Kline are similarly formal arrangements rather than ontological signatures.

These paintings then are depictions of a supernal yet natural being that is infinitely and profoundly patient, one that is absolutely motionless and completely pitiful and compassionate yet unmoving in its station of grace; what is pictured here occupies no space in the universe and is absolutely ideal in a Socratic or Platonic sense. These pictures portray a universal figuration that is unknowing of pain or hurt and which has not experienced the damage or psychic wounding come of time nor the mental anguish of being mortal and perpetually limited; yet their reality concerns nothing despite the fact that they are figures and not abstractions. The canvases are all different and yet the conceptual view that is being expressed is unified and it is as if the paintings only represent dissimilar yet identical dimensions of one discrete vision: an effect that draws upon further paradox.

In a way it is right that these canvases became so fugitive and evanescent and so evasive of human and temporal continuity for what they offer is a vision of the perfect and fully coherent: not simply of the perfect but of Being that is aware of and absolutely equal to the perfect. In this they are moral witnesses which we as viewers can barely attempt to consider: we become their flawed and mortal messengers or what classical Greeks referred to as the *théoros*. For timely creatures like ourselves the beautiful is only ephemeral and it is the kindness and terrific endurance in the life of Mark Rothko which has brought such a moment to fruition: for us, as we walk through and pause in an idealised mural room which he once made elsewhere and which has been recapitulated here in the Fogg.

Let us close with the final lines of Rothko's chapter on 'The Attempted Myth of Today' that appear in his book, *The*

Artist's Reality, published long after his death and in which he refers to art as "an ultimate unity"'. In this particular chapter he says that, "In our hope for the heroic, and the knowledge that art must be heroic, we cannot but wish for the communal myth again. Who would not rather paint the soul-searching agonies of Giotto than the apples of Chardin, for all the love we have for them?" In a previous chapter, 'Beauty', he says, "Both Leonardo and Dürer in their writings attested to a definite duality which they never quite manage to resolve. They both speak of painting being simply a mirror by implying that the mirror can not only mirror appearances, but that it mirrors the most profound aspects of appearances."

Finally, concerning the topic 'Beauty and its Apperception' the artist remarked that, "Insofar as we suggest that communicability is possible at all, we must accept some abstraction as a point of reference."

X

MAINE is a place unlike anywhere else that I have known in the Americas; it is the only location on this continent where I have felt at home and at rest, and where the experience of beauty is sufficiently satisfying that one seeks to pause and halt and to slow down all movement in order to sustain that appreciation. From that point of view it is a landscape where the perpetually transient figure of Diónysos is always ranging and unseen. Let us conclude now with a brief and material excursion in that faraway province to illustrate all of the above in firmer detail.

In *ultima* Maine I came upon a vision of simple visual and terrestrial truth which I grew to know and admire. It was a place of stern but gentle wildness, of dense and dim evergreen forests that stretched for tens of miles, dark and trembling with life and impassable shadow. It was neither spectacular nor sublime but intensely lovely and profoundly wonderful, for there the natural was the predominant force, unmediated by anything human except by a strange and marginal proto-neolithic sensibility which was inherent to the topography.

The region which my family and I visited was an area that is familiarly called Down-East, the most north-eastern coastal part of the United States which marches with the Canadian border. We had rented a small house upon the shore of a large and pleasant bay and before us, several hundred yards out, was an islet covered with spruce and fir where a pair of eagles nested and raised a single eyas. The voice of those two extremely large and kingly birds—*leucocephalus*—and the little enthusiastic scream of the eaglet when food was presented to it, threaded our days. They were the tyrants of the bay, great dark creatures with white heads and legs, gliding down to pluck fish out of the sea or soaring upon the thermals as sometimes the pair played in the air together circling far above us during hot afternoons.

Early on in the Seventeenth Century Maine was visited by
Europeans who hunted and fished, this was before the
pilgrim settlement of Plymouth in Massachusetts; the name
of the region came from France, the province of Anjou-
Maine. By the Nineteenth Century, shipbuilding, paper
manufacture, and lumbering were the vital industries, as well
as fishing. The little town of Harrington near where we stayed,
once constructed and launched vessels of three hundred and
fifty feet in length, full ships built of local timber. The
quarrying of granite is still a lesser business as outcrops of the
stone occur throughout the landscape.

Nowadays Maine is poor however—I think that it is, with
Louisiana or Missouri, one of the poorest states in the
Union—and it is only the fisheries that produce income along
with a modicum of summer tourism. There is modest
commerce and the state is scarcely populated: solitude and
silence characterise the place. Yet because of the forests and
the great physical antiquity of the region, and due to the
ubiquitous presence of the faultless sea with its vast Gulf
Stream tides, and because of the many pristine and unruffled
inland lakes, there is little sense of desolation or
impoverishment about the place. Virginal natural beauty
suffuses the visage of Maine, for there silence remains a great
metaphor, permeating the visual field with immense force.

Today the uninterrupted and continuous forest is all
secondary growth for almost everything was felled in the
Nineteenth and early Twentieth Centuries by the severe

predation of those rough lumberers. From a distance there is an aspect of pointed fir, spruce, pine, larch, cedar, juniper, and in places the brilliant white streak of birch shines out. Families of aspen, with their constant flickering tremor animate the scene. Bear and moose abound, as do small spotted deer.

I used to rise before the dawn in order to work at my desk as crows and garrulous jays noisily surrounded our little house during that early low light when the sun would rise and hover like a giant white star. Woodpeckers, with their *staccato* tapping sounds, and the quiet murmuring of wood pigeons softened the dawn air. There was one large and very shy pileated woodpecker, brilliant with a thick red crest, who would keenly hop about the tree trunks. Sometimes there would be the quiet barking of a fox for there was a den in the woods near to the house; there were also the voluble porcupines who would feed upon the aspen. Those long midsummer hours compressed sleep into its smallest possible unit as the days and brief nights merged into a semblance of timelessness.

At night, if there was no fog, the air would be pierced by the startling and liquid-golden flashes of fireflies. They supplied a disorienting perspective to the warm darkness with their weird punctuation, floating idly as they flared and fluidly burst upon the blackness. Their sparkling spontaneity fascinated my little son who would go out and walk the broad path which led to our cottage; for him it was a verification of a scene from one of the magical and wonderful books which he was then reading. Sometimes there would be an electric storm occurring far out to the east above Atlantic, and the sky would be repeatedly illuminated by a gigantic pulsing of soft plosive light, amber and pink and soundless.

Those mornings as I gazed out onto the island and bay watching the midsummer become topaz and cornelian as the sun rose above the distant forest and cast a zinc-coloured light to glitter voraciously and wonderfully upon the sea—if the tide was in—and upon the level muddy sands if it was out, those mornings for me possessed a sensibility that was almost transcendent. This was something which I had not felt nor witnessed for decades since I had lived alone in southern Greece and had used to watch the day arrive upon the ancient Aegean.

Such unique moments of pre-dawn and early dawn can be unqualified in their lucidity, particularly if they occur upon a marine surface, and I can recall sunrise at sea when I was sailing far out in Atlantic, and how remarkable those instants were for their saline freshness and breathless purity. It was the same at Harrington, and whatever I had been working on I would lay aside and simply watch the movement and variation of light as the planet rose out of the distance and assumed the vigour of day. The speed with which the sun moved up from the horizon was incredibly swift: one forgets how time actually possesses a physical and palpable motion and that there exists an actual pace to our lives. I always presumed that it was of a similar haste to the velocity of blood within our bodily channels.

Then the play and coruscation of light upon the water was exquisitely beautiful, particularly for its lack of substance and materiality and it seemed almost the envelope of life itself. That weightless glittering light, mercurial and metallic, was without dimension in a strong informal glare and the beauty was such that I merely sat and observed, wanting time to pause and for the scene never to diminish. Moon-rise, when the planet was full, was a similar experience, thoroughly ephemeral and yet astonishingly potent. I had not been witness to such events for many years, not since I had lived apart in a small stone dwelling in the southern Peloponnese; and there too, in those immaculate and enormous matutinal moments one could realise the profound beauty of life and paramount temperament without the brash intrusion of human presence. There was a truthful power to this experience of beauty and its nature without instinct, a strength that was uniquely compelling.

I would work for those long still hours before anyone else had wakened to the day and the only sound would be the old grand-mother clock striking the quarters and hours. Its chime was taken from the opening bars of an Eighteenth Century hymn which are now acoustically engraved upon my memory. Occasionally my wife would be woken by our baby daughter and would come in for a few minutes with the child in her arms, to sit and talk before returning to sleep some more.

Otherwise the house was noiseless. A few geese might fly past the building, low upon the water, mournfully crying out to each other, and once or twice I noticed an unusually large grey bird, perhaps a heron, gliding silently above the rocks.

I worked away at that old pinewood desk surrounded by various detritus which I had gathered on my walks and swims: shells and curiously dried starfish, feathers, a tiny model of a wooden half-boat that I had found on the shore. There were also two small silver and enamelled peacocks that my wife had once given me in the Kacch of Western Gujarat which I had brought with me. They seemed so out of place in that region where there was virtually no human nor civic culture, only an ancient terrain, mineral and forested, where the weather was the dominant figure. It seemed odd that the indigenous peoples in this place had been given the name of Indians by the white settlers, it was such a misnomer.

If the tide was low there might be the presence of small dark shapes upon the muddy flats of the bay: shell-fishermen who had walked out across the sands to dig for clams. They always appeared remote and unrecognisable, ghostly as they worked away for hours beneath an empty sky upon those endless stretches of tide. They were the only visible signs of life in that place without motors or wires. Beyond was an indefinite distance, a dark viridian horizon of trackless forest.

A few hours later the household would rouse itself and the day would proceed with a multitude of rites and habits. Our life in that cottage was like the solstitial humanity depicted in the pages of Tolstoi or Turgenev: formal, slightly quaint, with much conversation upon the subject of the day's climate and barometric change and the proximate state of the tide. There was a great reading and discussion of books as we were enclosed and separated from the rest of the world by a screen of flickering poplars and birches. Yet unlike those urbane Russians we hardly ever wore clothes and our nakedness— particularly during the hot canicular time—was a tactile enjoyment, especially during swims.

Our son assembled a small menagerie and natural history collection in the *gazebo* which soon became crammed with objects arranged upon a glass table along with various insects and reptiles, the pride of which was an old aquarium where he kept his snakes. He would often play with those creatures until one large one bit his finger and refused to release its jaws for several minutes. Humming-birds that had flown up from Brasil hovered about the netted walls of the *gazebo* feeding upon the nectar of petunias which grew in baskets hanging from the gables. A succession of dead frogs and tadpoles eventually caused too many tears and the menagerie calmly languished, its stones and bits of bark and flint testifying to the former passion.

In the evenings we used to sit outside on the terrace before the mosquitoes launched an assault and made us retire. Now and again the setting sun would crimson the trees of the island and the far-off forest and the vista was one of a bright flaming vermilion, golden and startling. One dusk as I was returning to the house from a late swim I noticed that the underside of the clouds above the settling sun had been coloured with a dazzling watery turquoise-blue like the innards of a shell, such was the vivid incandescent brilliance. Fitz Lane, who had painted the shipping in these parts in the late Nineteenth Century, captured some of that unearthly chromatic splendour on his canvases, but I had never actually experienced such a flamboyant and opalescent phenomenon.

The single focus of the day was the swim, which occurred when the tide was at its maximum height. The household business seemed to depend from that moment and all activities were prepared so that the swim would not be in any way inhibited or constrained. As our daughter was then still a baby, my wife and I used to plunge separately so that someone could always be on shore or at the house.

I ventured far out into the bay where it was solitary and completely open. Sometimes the skies above would be blue and pure, at other times they would be gunmetal grey and deeply convoluted, weighty with imminent rain. The weather systems in that region were unpredictable and changed with astonishing frequency; squalls would appear and pass over, crackling and booming with thunder and flooding us with their rapid deluge, then it would be suddenly blazing with heat, until a fog poured in and all would become visibly limited.

The gelid saline water of the green sea and the isolation were delicious and intoxicating, like a champagne or chartreuse, and the solitude out there was immense and without aspect. Once or twice a seal popped a black whiskery head out of the water, an instant that was always shocking and confusing for me. Often one of the eagles would spot a fish and would glide down on gaunt outspread wings from its lookout of lofty spruce and swoop upon the water to gather up the prey in its talons. At other times ospreys would be hovering and tense.

Swimming alone amid that great expanse of air and waves, especially if a fog was swirling about and obscuring the land, was like experiencing the emptiness of a human psyche: there was vacance and space and little else. It was a situation of original nakedness, without object or grammar or principle. Sometimes it could be slightly unnerving to undergo such a plenitude of sensory isolation, but it was always exhilarating. It was like approaching an extreme, knowing that one could go further and yet hesitating, for only death and seduction existed across that invisible margin. If evening was coming or a fog was circling about the bay I would feel a strange sense of the *unheimlich*, with the intimation of another world and that impossible expression. What was usually unmanifest in mundane life was more apparent out there in the tangible light.

During those midsummer days fogs would sweep in from off the sea, moving softly and steadily down into the bay. The meeting of warm canicular air and frigid gulf stream ocean would cause these sudden precipitations and the world would become abruptly dim and occlusive. On some occasions those silken heavy mists would continue for days and we would be clothed in a mysterious candid murkiness as if all of life had ended and there existed nothing else beyond our small and private household as we poised upon a terrestrial edge. There was only a slight pattering of dripping fog and at times the small eerie call of a loon, especially in the early morning.

Observing the approach of a fog was like watching some colossal sullen phantom unfurling itself upon the earth, unwrapping its slow protean and amorphous being as the dense white substance swept inland. The thoroughly atmospheric quality of fog only augmented the silence, a hush that would be occasionally perforated by the far-off and muffled whistle of eagles or the murmur of doves. The island would appear and disappear in the opaque light as if it were contracting and expanding in mass.

Swimming in those fogs was a strange and unearthly experience, like being far out in mid-Atlantic with no indication of life. Out there was an untouched and unqualified world with little sensory contact apart from small green undulations and their salt; perhaps a quick silvery fish would leap out of the water and submerge. There was no source of light to offer distinction, no horizon, only a chilly ocean and an obscure curling and condensed air and the delicate sound of rain falling upon the swells and splashing upwards into the wind.

Then, it was like the nerveless zero-nil of a solitaire mind, with psyche sealed and its veil raised. There were many grey apparitions out there and unheard wordless voices, the barest signs and hints of possible lives; they were neither threatening nor intimidating but only amplified the extraordinary magnitude of the situation, bordering upon what was potentially so unnatural and wholly without momentary instinct.

My most favoured walk was down the small peninsula by a path which led southward from our camp along a yellowish sand and gravel track, through the forest and towards the point. That walk soon became my daily habit, possessing what was almost an imperative or compulsion about it. There, at certain times of the summer we were pestered by plagues of black and green-fly and by crowds of starving mosquitoes and midges. I rambled footloose, shirtless and often barefoot about all those trails that threaded a narrow way among the trees. The oak cane which I took with me on those saunterings I had found in the house's cellar; it had been deeply scored with pencil, recording walks done in the early Twentieth Century about Massachusetts. Salem, Lowell, Springfield, and other towns, were all faintly inscribed, along with dates, most of them being in the Thirties.

The forest on either side of the path was always shadowless and dismal and a pungent odour of resin hung upon the air. I knew that it was alive with all kind of unseen creatures for I would spot their tracks and spoor in the dried mud that lined the road: cervines and numerous smaller quadrupeds. I often disturbed a young spotted doe and her fawn who would skitter away in perfect silence into the gloom of trees.

Primrose, ranunculus, vetch, swamp candles, and later, goldenrod, as well as a multitude of delicate grasses and stands of witch hazel, grew along the edge of the way. High bracken abounded and I used to pick the weird fronds to use as bookmarks; little scarlet strawberries and indigo blueberries sustained my wanderings whenever I felt hungry or thirsty.

Once on my sojourns I came upon a tiny cemetery deep in the woods where the remains of the Putnam family had been interred some two hundred years before; the slanting limestone of the grave-markers attested to the dates of their demise. Several young children were buried in that near-lightless and motionless space. It was a spot of great tranquillity and calm and my son and I returned to the place and took rubbings of the headstones for our notebooks.

It was a solemn and diminutive clearing, affluent in its reclusiveness and air of long repose, and although the light was veiled and shady it felt buoyant and ingenuous: there was nothing despondent nor grieving about the site and it lacked all melancholy. In fact the tone was one of great compassion and muted joy, a quietude of larch and balsam fir where no sunlight could reach with a slender beam or ray, such was the canopy of shadow. There was a patient ambience about the little graveyard and it was without flowers or birds and was sweetly mysterious, merely a slight memorial to the minor triumphs of human affection.

On another occasion, very near the point itself, I came across the vestiges of an old farm-house: the ruined and brown sandstone walls of a cellar and chimney where a pine now rooted and flourished. There were apple trees about the house and rock-roses grew with pink profusion; it was still obvious where pastures had once existed and a trace of boundaries could be seen despite the present overgrowing. The dried and broken wreck of a small boat lay beneath one apple tree, the timber of its ribs and hull cracked and splintered like an old rind.

There was a gentle charm about the spot, for its situation was perfect, and I imagined how a young couple must have found and loved the place and cleared the land to build their home and set out the fruit trees and flowers; perhaps they had a babe in arms with them. I could almost see them sitting on a ledge outside of their house at dusk as they spoke about their day's labour or the little child; as they watched rainbows reveal a spectrum above the bay or squalls of dark rain sweep across the water.

Once I spent a late afternoon wandering about those desiccated apple trees—now unproductive and hung with moss and lichen—and I had lain down upon the warm grass to sleep for a short while. When I awoke there were two eagles in the air above the bay—possibly the two from our island—playing on the currents, tumbling and crying, and I lay there in a luxurious daze following them in the sky. Ferns and strawberries flourished among the grasses and trillium about me. So much beauty seemed to be poised and unseen, a rare equilibrium had not deserted the spot although its human tenants had long ago fallen back to earth in their decease. I often wondered if they had been of the Putnam family.

Wherever I walked on those late afternoons I always seemed to find that my direction took me eventually southward and towards the point, a place where a large pink granite ledge covered the headland. There the panorama extended for more than two hundred degrees on either side, with an horizon of forest and further islands in the distance. There was one tiny islet in that bay where a solitary male eagle would sometimes pause during the hot hours. I would rest upon those old bare granitic rocks and watch the sea and air, transported by the unworldly vision of the place and for a while I could put aside my work and its effort. It was a place where sky and ocean intersected.

That site produced an emotion closely akin to mild *stasis* in me, such was my joy at the quiescence and untroubled solitude as I stretched upon those warm ancient stones and listened to the small sounds of water. Terns would be diving into the tide and gulls would be calling and crying in their peculiar frustrated fashion and I would watch the darting shearwaters and the busy little sandpipers flying so precisely in groups. A curious flotsam littered those sands and there was little human waste, unlike what one finds upon so many coasts of the modern world; it was clean. There was much seaweed at low tide and a mass of empty shells, clams and mussels. Whatever wood lay about, dry and waterless, was a deep pure grey in colour, come from years of marine itinerance.

Sometimes my family would join me later in the day and we would bathe, pleasantly nude in a cove, or lie upon the pebbly shore like an old hunter-gatherer group taking their ease whilst roving. Our solitude there possessed a stability in which the hours fused and blurred in a warm unending brightness come of the admixture of sunlight and northern ocean. A bevy of ospreys dwelled on a nearby headland and now and then one of them would jink in its flight and plunge downward into the waves to snatch a shining fish; perhaps a seal might float past, basking idly upon its back. Otherwise all was unremarkable, distinct only with light and the shimmering argent reflection of water.

Happiness and the longevity of happiness is an indefinable quality, something that coheres events and days rather than projecting its own aspect. It is a centripetal nucleus that persists in time as memorable and indelible, as about it experience attaches itself. During our months on that peninsula I was never specifically aware of any evident or overt happiness and the weeks ran by without significant graduation or sequence. Neither were there extraordinary moments, but rather, a gentle fidelity of days and nights which merged delicately with each other and were compounded into something for which I felt consciously and steadily grateful.

The simplicity of immediate kinship, of our genetic affinity and mental amity, was a structure which in itself—when time was trimmed of all unnecessary properties—afforded us great emotive pleasure. We did not realise it whilst we were resident there on that piece of the Maine coast but in retrospect it was apparent, how simply happy we were then; without desire and without anguish, glad in our daily human business and the enjoyment of an unclothed and shared being. A mutual life within that appealing and generous terrain of rock, forest, and sea, embraced us with simple benignance. Happiness is perhaps the impression of what can only be described as an *urgestalt*, which is at once both emotional and sensational.

The feelings which I experienced when singular at those bare rocks were of a radiant energy, parallel and akin to the experience of contemplation at its best, but without the mental effort which that must entail. Those great flat stones haunted me when I was not there; it was as if I were being driven or recalled and made to return, such was the strange impulsion by which the satisfaction of that place conveyed me throughout those tall bright blue days.

This was not the sublime for it lacked a grand natural impetus, but an experience of great and invisible beauty, a beauty that possessed the force of truth yet without words or reflex. It was an experience and an emotion that I had not known before, benevolent and overwhelming and yet thoroughly demanding and imperative in its earthliness. At times I felt as if I had been translated, for one was so vastly and yet so simply incorporated; but there can be no expression of this in words. It was as if there were ancient messengers in the air, inconscient and unaware and yet absolutely replete with knowing, hugely powerful and yet thoroughly compassionate in their demonstration of creative supernature.

My repeated and almost necessary observation of that view approached what was a state of immanence, without any need of the transcendent; it is this latter condition which I associate with the sublime. There was the sparkling sea and its movement whilst the great flat rocks themselves supplied the moments with an essence that was both unfamiliar and profoundly mediate. It was as if nature was open and unveiled, her bare self showing its matchless and imperishable validity and the ideation which this implied and enforced and which I then conceived. Those horizontal granite rocks were like unearthly vehicles of otherworldly form.

My nakedness upon that platform and before the sea, my skin touched by its light and breeze, was for an inadmissible period free of all the estrangement which civil and urban life requires. In time we are threshed and the grain removed and the old branches thrown aside; it was as if those instants had supplied me with a new autonomy to live as I was now informed and so possessed.

When the stable world of humanity loses its equilibrium and its movement becomes precessive and nutative, then—as with the Amor of *maestro* Dante—Diónysos will unexpectedly stand revealed and that appearance will cause the earth to resume a more appropriate and well-tempered circulation as one's human mind experiences another kind of life. Dionysos, who with closed eyes relentlessly witnesses the non-plurality of the world, then stands undressed. Let us now close this tribute to that unequalled and untimed figure with a brief anthem, telling of what we once saw and heard upon those bare rocks.

"A face of disturbing beauty, of morbid grace and vitality, covers itself so as not to be known. No, not mad but utterly quick, briefer than idea than flickering beams than light rising pink and raying above horizon, covering the earth with yellow planes, like cheek bones. Narcissus breed in the dim morning smelling of sex and death, anemone of black powdery hollows, iris with their delicate attraction proving the erotic not to be denied; white noon absolutely brilliant, followed by sleep and teeming silence, evening of wasps and vines, hot figs from the sunlight, cyclamen in the first rain then crocus, pale dusk and night, that curious darkness.

The dancer horned and masked above all this, drawing on the day, wheeling unseen, somewhere in ecstasy; compulsive music comes from those clay-parted lips, prophets singers lovers clothed in dust chant back a chorus, their gestures roused and animal till they vanish. Guide to sacrifice, guide beyond descent where no sense ever outlined a shape or name or white fleshy body, leader of those without visage, guide to the black wayless ways, the paths coiled tight, the flaming paths whose features are in shadow. The youthful dead succeed in train, laughing, suave, their manumission made them strange, strangers to the land below: all the loneliness of space is now themselves, each vivid mouth speechless, gasps with excitement.

Dawn day tranquillity, the sun crowned by a thin vague moon, serenity of twilight, fate; blood flows beneath the dancer's feet, an ever darkening song obscured in flashes, in bars of light that wander. At night the mask drops like a blind, the blood shows wet as dew, those cinerary eyes more potent than suns involve enough intention to incite the world to death and irreversible contempt; those eyes now cooled with hours veil themselves in constellation among high aerial breeze.

There is no sleep only birth, a soft anamnesis or breath; the mask is ever sealed lest its torrents dissolve and part, enervate the mere arterial mind, the not superhuman; flowers quietly celebrate the feasts, make small reflective shows of beauty. For those who have fallen or wish to follow, there is nothing but these words to the innocent: *I care not for death, for life, I only wait.*"

Kevin McGRATH (1951-2023) was born in southern China and educated in England and Scotland. He lived and worked in France, Greece, and India. He was an Associate of the Department of South Asian Studies and Poet Laureate at Lowell House, Harvard University.

Publications include, *Fame* (1995); *Lioness* (1998); *The Sanskrit Hero* (2004); *Flyer* (2005); *Comedia* (2008); *Stri* (2009); *Jaya* (2011); *Supernature* (2012), *Heroic Krsna* and *Eroica* (2013); *In The Kacch* and *Windward* (2015); *Arjuna Pandava* and *Eros* (2016); *Raja Yudhisthira* (2017); *Bhisma Devavrata* (2018); *Vyasa Redux* (2019); *Song of the Republic* (2020); *Fame* (2023); *On Friendship* (2024), *Dionysos: Nature Without Instinct* (2025), and *Causality In Homeric Song* (forthcoming 2025).

McGrath lived in Cambridge, Massachusetts, with his family.

GARAMOND - Garamond
Monotype Corsiva
Lucida Calligraphy
GILL SANS – Gill Sans
PERPETUA TITLING MT – PERPETUA TITLING

www.ingramcontent.com/pod-product-compliance
Lightning Source LLC
Chambersburg PA
CBHW020413130626
46549CB00006B/2544